Robert Cooper

Spiritual Experiences

Including seven months with the Brothers Davenport

Robert Cooper

Spiritual Experiences
Including seven months with the Brothers Davenport

ISBN/EAN: 9783337426675

Printed in Europe, USA, Canada, Australia, Japan

Cover: Foto ©Lupo / pixelio.de

More available books at **www.hansebooks.com**

SPIRITUAL EXPERIENCES,

INCLUDING SEVEN MONTHS

WITH THE

BROTHERS DAVENPORT,

BY

ROBERT COOPER,

"It has been the failing of fools in all ages to disbelieve whatever they could not account for."

"The Spiritualists, beyond doubt, are in the track that has led to all advancement in physical science; their opponents are the representatives of those who have striven against progress. . . . . . . What I deprecate is, not the wariness which widens and lengthens inquiry, but the assumption which prevents and narrows it."—Professor De Morgan.

"Testimony has been so abundant and consentaneous, that either the facts must be such as they are reported, or the possibility of certifying facts by human testimony must be given up."—Prof. Challis.

LONDON:

J. H. POWELL, PRINTER, GROVE ROAD, VICTORIA PARK, E.

CONTENTS.

CONTENTS.

SPIRITUAL EXPERIENCES.

CHAPTER I.

Electro-Biology.—First visit to a Medium.—
Bobby Burns.

AT the suggestion of numerous friends, I have been induced to publish an account of my experience with the Davenport Brothers; and in doing so, I have thought it well to preface it with my own experience in spiritual manifestations prior to my acquaintance with these mediums, and to trace, in a concise manner, my career in connection with the subject from the time of my first initiation to the time of their arrival in England; which I consider will not be without interest to my readers, especially those who are unacquainted with the facts of Spiritualism, to which my introduction was on this wise: —

In the year 1862, Mr. J.H. Powell visited

B

Eastbourne as a lecturer on Mesmerism. I was not altogether unacquainted with the subject, for some years before I had been present at a lecture on Electro-Biology, when the truth of that science was partially demonstrated in my own person. My limbs were made rigid; my eyes and mouth became fixed at the will of the operator; but some experiments that succeeded on other subjects did not succeed with me, and no other effects than those I have stated could be produced on myself. Regarding the matter simply as a psychological curiosity. I thought but little of it afterwards, until the arrival of Mr. Powell in his professional capacity, when I witnessed his experiments in public, and also at my own house. He endeavoured to mesmerise me, but without effect. He tried my children, but on one of them only could he succeed. This was my eldest daughter. Under his influence she soon became apparently unconscious, and fell into a state of coma; and in this state did a variety of things, her eyes being shut the whole time. At the operator's suggestion she went into the next room and played the piano in a style different to her own, and on becoming "herself again," stated that she was perfectly unconscious of what she had been doing, and quite ignorant of anything that had transpired.

With these experiments I was much struck; although at the time I saw but little importance in them. I had heard of Mesmerism being employed as a curative agent, but this, in a little book I had a short time before published (*Health in Nature,*) I had classed among the quackeries and delusions of the day.

It was, I think, on the occasion of this visit that Mr. Powell first broached the subject of

Spiritualism to me. I heard his tale with incredulity. He told me what he had seen at Madame Besson's, and described how tables were moved and how messages were obtained by means of raps. He said he had even seen a table suspended in the air without any visible support to sustain it there, and that his wife had been raised in her chair. Unlike most persons, who, on hearing for the first time such marvels described, pronounce them impossible, I did not actually do this; still I thought there must be some mistake about it. I remember well the feeling that came over me when I was alone, and began to reflect on what I heard. All that I had heard of apparitions, death tokens and such mysterious affairs—all the horrible things in Mrs. Crowe's "Night side of nature," which I had read some years before, and regarded as an excellent story book, flitted through my mind like a panoramic vision. After all, then, I said to myself, Supernaturalism may be true!

. Some months elapsed, and I called one day on Mr. Powell in London, and he proposed a visit to Mrs. Marshall. I consented, and we made our way to King Street, Holborn, where she then resided. I entered the house with some little feeling of trepidation, and was at once introduced to the lady in whose presence such wonderful things were said to occur. My first impressions of Mrs. Marshall, were, I confess, not very favourable. I expected to see in a person reputed to possess such extraordinary powers, some peculiarities which might be characteristic of these powers. Judge then of my surprise, at seeing an ordinary, stout and matronly old dame, just such an one as we may meet every day of our lives, without their attracting any notice whatever.   Mrs. Marshall, a niece of the old lady's, was also present, and struck me as possessing a much more sybil-like appearance, but in neither of them, either in appearance or manner, did I observe anything to awe or excite suspicion.   They both appeared to be frank, honest, and ingenuous, answering all my queries in a straight forward and unreserved manner.

At their request I and Mr. Powell placed our hands on a small round three-legged table, the ladies doing the same, and in less than a minute faint but distinct raps were heard on the table. The raps, I may observe, were not nearly so loud at that time as I have heard on my subsequent visits to Mrs. Marshall.   The table appeared to be endowed with vitality, and was raised in a curious manner.   I was invited to examine the table which I did by turning it upside down, but gained nothing by my examination.   It was evidently an ordinary table.   Mrs. Marshall said that a gentleman had been there a few days before and made experiments with a magnet, but could discover nothing by it.   Being re-seated we put various questions, which were answered affirmatively and negatively by the raps, one rap being understood to mean "No" and three raps "Yes." Mr. Powell was more successful in obtaining communications than myself.   The only thing of importance which occurred with reference to myself, was this: I had a few weeks before lost an uncle, with whom I had been on intimate terms, and I was one of his executors. I asked if his spirit was present.   Three raps in reply.

"Will you spell your name?"

Three more raps   I expected the name Colman

to be spelt, instead of which, the letters J O H N were signalled, and then C O L —, but nothing more could be obtained. My relation's name was Colman; this certainly puzzled me, and any thing in the shape of a solution seemed impossible. Mr. Powell, I felt sure, knew nothing of my relatives, and never had heard of this uncle or his death. At our request the table was lifted up, and then a succession of raps on the floor seeming to die away in the distance was understood to mean that the spirits had departed. This terminated the *Séance*, which was considered to be very unsatisfactory; so much so, that on my offering a small sum to Mrs. Marshall in acknowledgment of her services, she declined to accept it, alleging that I had seen nothing. To compensate, however, for my want of good fortune, I was told of a great many marvels that had occurred, and shewn a photograph of a handkerchief which had been tied up in a curious knot by the spirits.

As Mr. Powell's experiences were more satisfactory on this occasion than my own, I extract his account of the *Séance*, also of a previous one, from his *Facts and Phases of Spiritualism*, which contains some of my early experiences not recorded here:—

"At one sitting rappings from invisible knuckles would be felt and heard upon the legs of my chair. The next minute on the ceiling and in all parts of the apartment the same mysterious sounds would distinguish themselves.

Generally, at the close of the sittings, the departure of the spirits was preceded by an indistinguishable number of raps, loud at first, then gradually faint and fainter, until, like echoes on a hill, they fainted away in the echoing distance.

Make yourself happy. Believe in God--and sentences with a *God bless you* at their end, were frequently spelt out. Sometimes letters were jumbled together
in such uncouth order as to make neither sense nor
reason.

As a specimen of defective orthography I present
the following verse, which came to me from a spirit
who persisted in presenting himself as " Robin Burns."
I had desired to know if the spirit of any poet would
communicate with me. The table in the usual manner
gave eager response in the affirmative.

" Who is it ? Will you spell your name ?" was my
compound enquiry. Three knocks. The letters
rapped out were *Robin.* " Robert Burns ?" The
table knocked and tilted an affirmative, with evident
satisfaction.

Of course I felt honoured, and what person with
poetic sensibilities would not ?

A lucky thought took possession of my brain. I
would get the Bard of Scotia to improvise a verse or
two—a talent for which he was famous in his life-
time.

" Will Robin kindly give us a verse or two of
poetry ?" I asked, with due solemnity of tone, and a
strong disposition for an affirmative response.

The table's three decisive knocks sent a thrill of
pleasure through me.

" Now, please, let's have them."

The table commenced beating affirmative knocks
with its foot on the floor, marking on the alphabet
the following letters :—

O Cotland thy loks and thy mountains
Thy woods and heather so wild—
Thy waters from nature's pure fountains
I have dı ank from when I was a child.

ROBIN.

" Is that all ?—One knock.

" But you don't pretend to say that you are the spirit of the great Scottish Songster ?"

The table thundered out three knocks, with a suddenness almost electrical.

Surely Burns could spell correctly, and present a better specimen of his genius than this, I thought.

The quickness, however, with which the words were spelt out, and the rythmical effort of the lines obtained in the manner described tended to, puzzle me much.

On a future occasion, sitting at the same table with my friend, Mr. Cooper, whom I had prevailed upon to witness some spiritual phenomena, I invoked the pretended spirit of Burns with the view to obtain some more poetic effusions. The following is a correct copy of the second verse elicited by means of the alphabet. This came without defective orthography :—

Thy balmy breath of the morning,
As it comes upon life-giving wings,
When the lark from her nest is up-soaring,
What joy to the heart it brings.

" Is that all ?"—One knock responded.

" Then proceed."

The letters were deliberately signalled out, forming the words *Bobby Burns*.

There was a general laugh. The table seeming to take up the chorus.

" Robert Burns you mean ?"

The table thundered *No*.

The laughter only became more boisterous. The " Robert " was asserted to be meant by us all and not the " Bobby." But the table wouldn't have it. It rapped assent every time the word " Bobby " was mentioned, and persisted in refusing to allow the more respectful name of " Robert " to pass without kicking out its stubborn negatives.

There was a lapse of several weeks between the sittings, which gave me the opportunity of obtaining the
two verses above quoted.   Yet in the theme and the
word " Thy," commencing the first line of the last
verse, the relation of the two verses is visible.   A
slight alteration and halt in the metre give evidence
of a want of finish ; still, there is the rudiment of
design in the whole.

Nothing worthy of further note passed at this sitting,
except that Mr. Cooper obtained a communication
from an alleged spirit, who spelt out *John Col*, and by
no manner of solicitation could be prevailed upon to
knock the additional *m a n* out, which would have
made the name of a deceased relative complete."

CHAPTER II.

Is it Satanic ?—Physical Manifestations—An Engineer's Testimony—Spirit Writing—Seances at Home—Strange table Movements—Professor Faraday.

The above events took place in November, 1862, and I saw nothing more of the kind 'till the following Summer. My experience was then further extended; the particulars of which may be gathered from the following letter I addressed to the *Spiritual Magazine* :—

Sir,—With your permission, I will give your readers an account of the little experience I have had in Spiritualism. The subject had engaged my attention from time to time, but I, as most persons are apt to do, regarded the whole thing as. a myth. I had occasionally seen accounts of wondrous doings in news-papers ; these I looked upon as so much food provided for the lovers of the marvellous. I read the article in the *Cornhill Magazine*, and for the first time heard of a "floating medium." This affair though perplexing to the mind, was disposed of by supposing that the persons present were deceived by the events taking place in the dark. I next had the direct testimony of a friend, in whom I could place implicit confidence, that he himself had seen some wondrous things, one of which, was a table standing in mid-air, untouched by any one present. Inexplicable as all

this appeared to me, I was, nevertheless, reluctant to
give in my adhesion to statements so contrary to
general experience, and for the accomplishment of
which, the established laws of nature must be set
aside, or new or unknown ones brought into operation. The subject, was however, soon after, brought
more practically under my notice. About three
months ago a young gentleman was staying in this
town, and Spiritualism was incidentally mentioned to
him ; he said that some years ago, when table turning
was in fashion, he had sat at a table and seen it move.
He was asked to try again. He did so, and very decided movements soon took place, but nothing more
was done on this occasion. The next night I was
invited to attend, and after being seated about ten
minutes, the table seemed as if endowed with life and
intelligence. It responded to questions by giving the
usual affirmative or negative raps with the leg. An
alphabet was extemporised, and immediately a remarkable and *apropos* sentence was spelt out, purporting to come from an old clergyman who had died a
few weeks before. It will be well to mention that this
gentleman had held the idea, so long prevalent among
the clergy, that if there is anything in Spiritualism at all
it is Satanic, and that it should on no account be practised. He had given me a pamphlet to read, written
by an Irish clergyman of the Name of Nangle, plau-
sibly setting forth that Spiritualism was of the devil.
"There," said he very assuredly, "that will show you
where it comes from." Well, this old gentleman
having announced himself, was asked if he had anything to communicate, and without hesitation there
was spelt out—
When I was alive, I did not believe in Spiritualism.
"Is it Satanic ?"
No.
"Then good spirits as well as evil spirits are engaged in these manifestations ?"
Yes.
The names of deceased friends were spelt out on

this occasion, but no farther communication was made, the chief interest centering in the movements of the table, which were remarkable to us on account of their novelty, we never having seen anything of the kind before. The next evening the same description of manifestations took place; some questions of a theological character were answered, and the movements of the table exhibited greater power. An interesting circumstance occurred which is worth recording. A child was taken from a cradle and placed upon the table, which at once proceeded to rock with a cradle-like motion. We were expecting the table to go along the ground, as we had seen it on the previous evening, when a person mounted it. On retiring to rest our medium was greatly disturbed by rappings, which continued the greater part of the night, and he could not be induced to attend a *Séance* again. Not liking to abandon our experiments at so early a stage, we tried among ourselves, and had the satisfaction to find that two of our party were mediums, though not very powerful ones. The movements of the table, however, increased in power on repetition, and were produced more readily. I have frequently seen at my own house, a heavy man raised on the table, the only contact with it being our fingerends lightly resting on it. We get questions promptly answered affirmatively or negatively, but an appeal to the alphabet is seldom successful. The name of a lady has been rapped out as a medium, but as she cannot be persuaded to join in our experiments, we have not been able to test her mediumship.

Here are fair spirits—was on one occasion spelt out; this, on inquiry, we found to mean that the spirits present were *good* spirits.

At this stage of our proceedings, a gentleman (a civil engineer) requested permission to see our experiments. He witnessed them, and was much struck with what he saw, and became so much interested in the matter that what we could show him was not enough; to use his own words, he wanted to "see the hands."

I recommended him to Mrs. Marshall in London, of whom I had heard. He went, and sent me the following report :—

"Knockings and scratchings were heard about the room and on the table. Questions were promptly answered by loud raps on the table. The name of my sister was correctly spelt out; and the place where her remains are buried, and several questions were correctly answered. After this, the table rose about three feet in the air, and remained so for several seconds, in defiance of the laws of gravitation. I watched the movements with great earnestness and care, and could discover no appearance of fraud."

On receiving this account, I made a journey to London to see and judge for myself. On arriving at M.'s I found a party of about six, among whom was a lady receiving a long communication from her father ; a page or two of which she read for our edification. On putting the usual question, whether there was any spirit present, the name of *Mary Cooper* was rapped out, the alphabet being pointed to by an American gentleman, who happened to be present. Not recollecting any one of that name, I enquired who it was, and was answered *Grandmother*. She stated that she died about thirty years ago, and was my guardian spirit. I have since ascertained the year of her death to be 1833. She died when I was very young, and my parents having died previously, the responsibility of my care devolved upon the old lady, who always manifested great interest in my welfare. How wonderful that she should thus spring forth to light again at a time when I had all but forgotten that such a person had ever lived ! At this stage of the proceedings a friend, who accompanied me, asked if any manifestations of a different kind to those we had yet seen could be produced.

Yes.

"Can any spirit present give us direct writing ?"

Yes.

Hereupon I placed upon the floor some note paper

and a pencil, and on taking it up, about two minutes after, the name *Mary Cooper* was legibly written, in a bold free hand. I marked the paper previous to putting it down. I afterwards placed on the table a photograph, enclosed in an envelope, of a dear, deceased relative; her name was instantly spelt out accompanied by the benedictory words *Joy be with you.* The American gentleman before alluded to, now began singing, which seemed to increase the movements of the table (a 4-feet loo,) and it rose fairly from the floor to the height of about a foot. The rappings now were not confined to the table, but were all about the floor, which shook with a tremulous motion, resembling, as one present observed, an earthquake.

I attended again a short time afterwards, when the same description of phenomena occurred. Singing was again introduced, and on this occasion, the table, a smaller one than that before used, rose in the air, and remained there with a vibratory motion till the close of each verse, when it descended and rose again at the commencement of the next. The spirit of Dr. Esdaile was invoked, and on being told that he was present, the gentleman requested that he would, if possible, mesmerise him. The table hereupon rose from the ground and assumed the actions of a mesmerist in making the usual mesmeric passes; the imitation was perfect. Dr. Esdaile, the celebrated mesmerist in India, was well known to the gentleman who made the request. On another occasion, a military gentleman, threw a handkerchief on the floor; the alphabet was called for, and the words

We have made you a pretty present,

were rapped out. On taking up the handkerchief, it was found to be tied in knots.

Such are some of the striking incidents I saw at Mrs. M.'s; and coupled with what I have witnessed in my own house, where anything like deception or imposition is out of the question, they appear to me so conclusive, of the truth of the spiritual theory, and

indeed, so impossible on any other theory than
that of spiritual agency, that I unhesitatingly
give my testimony to its truth, and I believe it destined, under Providence, as the great antidote of
materialism, to work marvellous results in the future
of humanity. After what I have seen, I can no more
doubt the existence of spirits and of these spiritual
phenomena, than I can the sunshine that warms and
irradiates the earth ; and I feel assured that all who
will take the trouble to investigate the matter properly, will very soon be of the same conviction.—I
remain, &c.,   R. Cooper.
2, Terrace, Eastbourne, Nov, 9, 1863.

For several weeks we continued to hold *Séances*
in my house almost every night, the medium
being Mrs. Hicks, and as I never objected to
visitors being present, a great number of persons
witnessed our experiments, most of whom, went
away with the impression that there was "something in it." But a great diversity of opinion
prevailed with respect to the cause. Some were
in favour of electricity ; some attributed it to an
undeveloped force in nature ; some only gave vent
to such expressions as "very extraordinary!"
"very curious certainly.!" &c., while one gentleman, not overgifted with brains, pronounced it
"very clever!" and said he thought there must
be quicksilver in the table. He, however, on his return home, made some experiments on his own table
with his own family and, to his surprise, found his
mahogany to move about in the same manner he
had seen mine, which was of course, a practical
refutation of his quicksilver theory. The most
remarkable phenomena produced through Mrs.
Hick's mediumship were powerful table movements. Not only would the table be moved, but

a heavy man seated on it would be lifted up. The table generally used was a large loo table weighing about eighty pounds, and this was moved in two or three instances without the contact of any person. The first time we witnessed this phenomenon, we were sitting round a smaller table than that generally used, when, noticing that the table was endowed with great force, I suggested that we should draw away from it, which was done, one of the party stooping to see by the pattern of the carpet, whether it moved in the slightest degree. I said "will the spirits bring the table to me?" upon which it came straight up to me. I then drew back as far as I could get, the others retaining their places; I then asked for the table to be brought to me again, and immediately it came right up to me. This experiment was repeated three or four times, and on a gentleman coming into the room we told him what had occurred, and, standing with his elbow resting on the mantelpiece, he witnessed a repetition of the experiment. In this case the floor was carpeted, the table without castors, and the gas fully burning, and only five persons present, all of whom were perfectly satisfied that the table was moved by no known physical agency. Sometimes a larger table was used with the same results, and the tables give evidence of the rough treatment they have experienced in dislocated legs, loose castors, &c.

On one occasion an incident of an amusing character took place. Two sceptical gentlemen were present and were seated at the table opposite each other. The table began tilting in the direction of the side at which they were sitting. They were so absorbed in the movements that it did not oc cur to them, that, if the table was moved by any visible agency, it must be done by themselves. Mr. Hicks, who was present, called their attention to the fact by making the remark "Look how you are moving the table?" "It is not I" says one "I do not move it." says the other. "It must be one of you," rejoined Mr. Hicks. "I tell you it is not me" they both said with some warmth. It "must be, for there is no one else to do it" added Mr. Hicks, in a serious and emphatic tone, on which they both became very indignant, and were not duelling almost numbered with the things of the past, I doubt not but a challenge would have been considered necessary to satisfy their wounded honour. To moderate their anger, Mr. Hicks finished the affair by coolly saying "That is probably what you would have said of me if I had been seated where you were."

I once made an experiment with a table which I think worth recording. I placed a half cwt. weight on the centre of the table. I then placed my hands on the table and tried to pull it down, this I found I could do by dint of considerable effort. I then placed the weight further from me, and I then found it impossible to move; but the table at my request began tipping towards me without the slightest effort on my part. Considering that this experiment upset the involuntary muscular theory of Professor Faraday I wrote to him on the subject, giving him a detailed account of my table experiments, making particular reference to the last with the weighted table, and concluded my letter, in which I said nothing about spirits, by asserting my belief of the entire absence of trickery as we were a party of investigators anxious to arrive at the truth. To my letter I received the following courteous reply, which forms a good companion-letter to the one he sent to the Davenports, which will be found in another part of this book.

The Green, Hampton Court.

25, September, 1863.

" SIR,—I hasten to acknowledge your letter, for I freely admit my belief that you are perfectly sincere and truthful in your account of experiments. Nevertheless I refer you to my former letter for my answer now.

Your observation that you have the greatest confidence in your colleagues makes me smile when I call to mind certain investigations that have come to my knowledge in former cases.

I do not doubt your competency to check the facts if you are willing to work with an unbiassed mind ; but I decline to enter upon the matter.

Very truly yours,

M. FARADAY.

R. Cooper, Esq.

CHAPTER III.

The lock of hair.—A new medium—Animated Music stool— Writing — Autograph fac-similes — Unknown tongues—Familiarity with the Supernatural—Messages.

At this stage of our proceedings my two daughters returned from school for their holidays. They knew nothing of Spiritualism. We held a *Séance* at night at which they were present. The usual manifestations took place and naturally excited their surprise. Nothing, however, very particular took place at the *Séance*, but on their going to bed, a very extraordinary circumstance occurred. A box brought with them from school had been emptied of clothes and was used for keeping their hats in. On opening this box a coil of their mother's hair, partially enclosed in an envelope, was observed to be lying on the hats. An exclamation of pleasurable surprise attended the discovery of the lost hair. But how came it there, that was the mystery. The circumstances attending its loss were as follows. When home for their holidays the previous midsummer, a little dog had taken advantage of the hair being left about and used it as a thing to sport with. The hair was much ruffled by the treatment. It was, however, put to rights in the best way possible and placed in a workbasket. Soon after it was suddenly missed, and notwithstanding a search being made in all likely and unlikely places, no trace of the lost treasure could be found, and the affair was, I may say, forgotten until the incident above related occurred. I made inquiries of every one of the household, which consisted of my family and two servants. They all emphatically denied any knowledge of the hair, and I have no reason to doubt them. The servants, we had at the time, had only been with us a few weeks and knew nothing of the lost hair. The affair was an entire mystery. So I said " We will ask the spirits about it; perhaps they can tell us something." I took the opportunity when next communicating with them to ask if they could tell us anything about the hair.

I had it. Was the reply.

"What did you take it for? My daughter asked.

Because you were careless.

"When did you take it?" Was the next query."

June.

" Did you hide it in the house or take it right away?" I asked.

I took it away. Was the answer.

At the time I regarded this manifestation as quite unique, but I have since heard of many similar and equally extraordinary occurrences.

A few nights after, (it was New year's Eve) we held another *Séance,* and I then noticed that the table moved when no one touched it but my eldes daughter. This led me to inquire if she were a medium; to which I received an affirmative reply. The spirit of my wife purported to be the

c 2

communicating spirit, and gave us each a short and characteristic communication. All had received a message but my youngest little boy, when a pause in the proceedings suddenly occurred.

" Won't you say something to me"? he meekly but earnestly said. At first there was no response, but on the request being repeated, the words :—

Come and be with me, were rapped out.

I hid them from the child as well as I could, at least the latter part of the sentence, lest it might excite alarm and apprehension in his youthful mind, and Mrs. Hicks was so overcome at the occurrence as to shed tears, and left the table, saying she would have no more to do with it. A gloom fell upon our little party and it broke up in silence, impressed with the feeling that an import was attached to the message, which fortunately has not up to this time been realized.

The day following was the 1st, of January 1864. We were seated round the fire after dinner when the events of the previous evening came to my recollection. The message of apparently ominous import had produced an uncomfortable feeling in my mind, but I was too much interested in the subject to give it· up, as Mrs. Hicks seemed disposed to do, and remembering the circumstance of the table moving under my daughter's reputed mediumship, it occurred to me to test it alone. So, as a first experiment, I desired her to place her hands on a small music stand (known as a Canterbury) and soon had the satisfaction of seeing it exhibit the same kind of motion we had so often seen in the table. It went round the room—there was no holding it. It lifted and struck the floor with its legs, and the next day vibrated with such rapidity that its shape was indefinable. I procured an alphabet and pointed to the letters, at which it rapped, but when the letters were placed side by side they formed only an unmeaning jumble. A succession of trials produced no better results. I then said "perhaps you are a writing medium," and placed a pencil in my daughter's hand. After holding it about a minute she exclaimed, "It's going, I can't help it." I looked at the paper but there was nothing but a string of m's and n's. "Try again," I said. This time the hand moved slower and the words *Sister love* were legibly written in a style entirely different to her own. Her mother's name was next written, followed by the sentence *I love you, and want you to love God.* A peculiarity in the writing was that all the tail letters, whether above or below the line, were about three times their proper length. John Colman, to whom reference has already been made, next wrote his name, adding, *I see you, so I do,* and *I often think of you all.* But the most striking incident that occurred was this. The name "Mary Cooper," was written in a peculiar old-fashioned style ; this was the name of my grandmother already alluded to in the letter to the *Spiritual Magazine.* I remembered she had given me a book some thirty years before in which she had written her name. I searched the next day and found it, and in comparing her original autograph with the one now produced they were seen to be almost identical. The formation of the letters was nearly exact, the principal difference being in respect to size ; the involuntary writing was the largest of the two. This signature was afterwards produced several times. My daughter, I am quite sure, had never seen the original autograph, 'and had never, I believe, heard of this grandmother. Here, then, was a wonderful fact, impossible to be accounted for on any known principle of physics or metaphysics. Scores of persons have seen the two writings and all agree in their wonderful similarity.*

The writing faculty was cultivated and became more developed. The letters gradually assumed their natural proportions and other fac-similes of the departed were produced, also specimens of chirography entirely strange to us. And to set the matter beyond all doubt—that the writing was not the product of the medium's own brain, she wrote in languages she knew nothing of; these were sometimes written with great rapidity. I believe I could enumerate a dozen different languages she has written; the very names of some of which were unknown to us at the time, and it was only by submitting them to competent persons that we obtained a clue to what they were, and one or two specimens we could not get deciphered at all. The following are the languages we have had writing in. French, Dutch, Italian, German, Russian, Latin, Assyrian, Chinese, and Spirit language, so-called by the spirits themselves, and a specimen said by the spirits to be Egyptian and Persian.

In conseqence of Mrs. Hicks declining to take part in our *Séances* we discontinued holding them in what may be called a systematic manner, and instead, used to get communications from our

---

* Fac-similes are published in Powell's Facts and Phases of Spiritualism.

spirit friends at all hours of the day. They appeared to be always present, and would make their presence known sometimes when we were not thinking about such matters. Thus at dinner they would move the table or cause our chairs to vibrate. On one occasion my daughter went into the drawing-room to practise the piano, and while so doing the stool on which she sat began rocking about. Though alone, she was not at all alarmed but simply said " let me finish my practising and then you may rock me about as much as you like."

Why even our children would not be alarmed at supernatural occurrences if they understood them and were familiarised with them. It is the mystery in which the subject is involved and the semi-admission of its reality that does the mischief, producing the fear and apprehension that exists in the minds of the multitude.

In the following remarkable passage, Judge Edmonds testifies to the same effect on the youthful members of his family.

" Only a few evenings ago, I was sitting alone in my library, profoundly thinking upon a great moral question on which I had some perplexing doubt. I looked up, and my only brother, who died about a year ago, stood by my side, within three feet of me. He told me he came as the messenger of a higher intelligence to solve that doubt; and he did so, with an expression of countenance, a manner, and in language, entirely characteristic. We had a brief conversation on the subject, and as soon as he perceived that I understood him, he vanished. I saw him as plain as I ever saw him in life, and if I could ever identify him I could then. Now if this was not the spirit of the departed, what was it? and whence came the clear wisdom of his teaching, far as it was beyond my capacity to originate? Fifty years ago this would have been a ghost story, and the silly education of my childhood would have caused me to be frightened; and now it has been of such frequent occurrence with so many people, and under so many various circumstances, and it has come to be so well understood, that it excites no alarm, no agitation, even. *Why, even our children laugh and play with the spirits!* Men believe in the Bible! Then they believe that in the olden time mortal men saw the spirits of the departed. Who was it that Peter, and James, and John, saw with Jesus on the mountain? And who was it that John saw in the Revelations, but one of his brethren, the prophets? And wherein, pray, has the nature of man so changed, that what was possible to him eighteen hundred years ago, is not possible to him now."

I confess I used to be somewhat timid in these matters, but now having become familiarised with them, they occasion me no alarm. I think but little more of conversing with spirits than with mortals. We have only to realise the idea that spirits are disembodied human beings, and all cause for fear vanishes.

To return to my subject, sometimes my daughter when seated in a chair would be thrown back, and in this position would resist considerable force to push it forward. Sometimes at night the spirits would make a noise as if stones were thrown through the window and then fell on the floor. This was heard by the governess as well as by my daughter, both occupying the same room. On two occasions I was awoke just as I was falling off to sleep, by loud knockings; the first night on the door, the next night on the window. On hearing the sounds I sat up in bed, somewhat alarmed, but could hear nothing more. The next day when communicating with the spirits I referred to the knocking of the previous night, telling them I did not approve of being disturbed in that way, when they said, *We were going to speak to you, but you were afraid.* I sometimes obtained communications by getting my daughter to place her hand on a small table. If she happened to be reading at the time she did not leave off; I would then take the alphabet to another part of the room and point to the letters, and in this way long sentences were obtained, the letters being indicated by three movements of the table. I give a few specimens obtained in this way.

Mary, I hope you try to love God, and that you make a happy home for your dear papa, and brothers and sister.

Heaven is a beautiful place, we sing lovely songs and play on golden harps.

These two sentences were also given by the tilting of the table and addressed to my children.

Kate is here, and she loves you very much.

When you go to bed pray to God.

The following is the longest communication I ever obtained by this mode and was given with great rapidity and without the slightest error :—

Mary, I hope you love God, and try to make your Papa happy. Love Ada, Ernest, Archy and Ion. Will you write to aunt Marion and tell her that Spiritualism is true ? Go and tell aunt H——y that I have communicated to you, and tell her that I wish her to come and see me and be convinced. Go and tell her that I will come to the table and say what I

*have to communicate, and we will tell her many things
about Spiritualism.   Go and see her directly, for she
must be told as soon as possible, or she will not believe
what you say.*

In the above a desire is expressed by the spirit
to communicate with her relatives.   This is what
we may suppose a spirit would naturally wish to
do when it had found a way of communicating.
For about a week these importunate requests continued to be made and then ceased altogether,
for though couched in most earnest terms they
were unavailing in inducing the parties addressed
to "come and see and be convinced," so great
was the prejudice against the subject; they did
not deem it right, they averred, to disturb their
sweet sister's repose: speaking as though the
spirits of the departed were sleeping in the grave
along with mouldering dust.   To such a poor,
pitiable condition has modern orthodoxy reduced
the faith of its devotees !

CHAPTER IV.

Lectures — A Clergyman's Letter — Ghost stories — Molly Downing — A Visit from Prince Albert.

Thus matters went on for about a fortnight when I happened to meet a medical gentleman who had been present at our *Séances* and witnessed the manifestations through Mrs. Hick's mediumship, and expressed himself much astonished at them. I recounted what had since taken place and he then suggested that a lecture should be given on the subject. " Well," I replied, " Why don't you give one? " No," said he, " you are the proper person to do that." "Well, I will consider the matter," I added. Upon the strength of this and receiving messages from the spirit-world, urging me to "publish and plead the cause of Spiritualism," I determined to give the public an account of my experiences, and with that object announced two lectures at the Assembly Rooms.

It is not to be surprised at in a little town like Eastbourne, where everything that happens is known from one end to the other, that our doings should have been fully canvassed, and that excitement should run high. Of course, there was, as usual, a great diversity of opinion on the subject;

the doctors and the *quasi* scientific, pronouncing it all humbug and delusion, while the religious folk, with the clergy at their head asserted, like the priests asserted of the Jackdaw of Rheims, that "the devil was in it."

One learned disciple of Hippocrates, living in a neighbouring town, gravely questioned me with regard to my regimen and general habits; did I drink much? did I sleep well, and was I troubled with dreams? Very few in the parish but what were tolerably conversant with our doings, since we made no secret of them, and never shut the door against any inquirer.

One of the leading families of the town took up the matter very warmly, said it was nothing but "witchcraft revived," and threatened Mr. Hicks to do him all the injury they could in his photographic business if he persisted in the practice of Spiritualism. This unseemly conduct called forth the following sharp and well-merited rebuke from a clergyman, at that time connected with the University of Cambridge.

DEAR SIR,—I am much obliged to you for your two letters and the interesting information they contained. Have you ascertained, by reference to any Persian scholar, whether the writing said to be Persian, really is so.

I sincerely hope that your paper is increasing ts circulation. I sent a copy of one number (of which you sent me two or three) to my friend, Professor——, with whom I had a long conversation on the subject. He and his wife seemed much interested in it; they had been reading De Morgan's book "From Matter to

Spirit," and he was quite ready to examine into the question *fairly* and *candidly*. What a contrast to the conduct of the " Evangelical party" at Eastbourne, whose persecution of poor Mrs. Hicks is most disgraceful. I have half a mind to write something on the folly of their proceedings, for publication either in your paper or as a separate tract ; but I fear it would be only a waste of time and money. It is of no use to argue with such imbecile bigots, whose ignorance of the whole thing is on a par with their unchristian spirit in thus venting their petty malice on persons whose moral character is as good and (perhaps better) than their own. But Spiritualism is going through exactly the same ordeal as Christianity at the first. The blind and conceited Pharisees of the present day will *not* examine the claims of the new faith, and *will* persecute all who dare to do so. The time will come when the clergy will discover what a set of fools *they* have been—just as Dr. Elliotson is doing, in denying or rejecting the evidence of so many thousands, or ascribing to Satan what they cannot deny to be real. " Blind leaders of the blind," now as of old. The Rector of this parish saw a number of your paper on my table. when he paid us his first visit. He knew nothing of the subject, and evidently did not care to know anything ; very likely he set me down as a " dupe," but he is too much of a gentleman to begin raving against the poor " dupes," as your Eastbourne " Evangelicals " are doing.

I shall always be glad to hear how you are going on.

Yours truly,   ——

Two or three other circumstances also occurred at the time that tended materially to increase the interest in the matter. An old woman by the name of Downing was reported by several trust-

worthy witnesses to have appeared in bodily form
—"in the habit as she lived"—after her death,
which had taken place some six weeks before;
and mysterious rappings were nightly heard about
her dwelling.   These things are strenuosly main-
tained by the parties who witnessed them to the
present day.   An old pensioner had also appeared
to his wife who was at another part of the town at
the time, and on her return home she found her
husband lying dead on the floor in his shirt,
having broken a blood vessel. Mrs. Griffin, in
whose house the apparition appeared, told
me that the woman spoke to her at the time,
about what she had seen, and impressed with the
idea that all was not well, she returned home
sooner than she otherwise would have done.   A
strange revelation made through mediumship,
clearing up the mystery attached to an old
malthouse, reputed for many years to be haunted,
also transpired at this time.   In this case the
spirit reiterated his unhappy condition, and at
length disclosed the cause of his unhappiness.
This was an injury done to another in his life-
time. A reconciliation was ultimately effected and
the hauntings gradually ceased. The most curious
part of the affair is this; the spirit gave his name
and the number of years he had been in the spirit-
world, (seventy and a half years,) which was found
to agree with the date of the death of a former
owner of the premises as recorded on his tomb-
stone in the parish churchyard.   None of the parties concerned knew anything of the history of the
building so many years ago.*

---

* Full particulars of these cases are given in Powell's Facts
and Phases of Spiritualism.

Fifty other ghost stories and such like affairs obtained currency, in fact everybody had a tale to tell of some marvellous event either occurring to himself or somebody he knew. All these circumstances combined caused excitement to run high, and therefore it is not altogether a matter of surprise that the hall on the night of my lecture should have been filled with a dense crowd. A great number of those present were neighbours of the old woman whose apparition had been seen, and to this circumstance I was somewhat indebted for the overflowing audience I was honored with.

I had proceeded with my lecture for about half-an-hour without interruption; but now signs of impatience began to be manifested and a cry for Molly Downing was set up. For some time I paid no attention to these demonstrations, but at length I found it necessary to appeal to the audience to give me a hearing. I was then for the first time made to understand that the malcontents had come to the lecture under the impression that they were going to see the redoubtable Molly Downing " raised " upon the platform, after the style, I presume, of Pepper's Ghost. I explained to the audience that I had simply announced a lecture and had no intention of illustrating it with manifestations; on their persisting in expressing their dissatisfaction, saying they " wanted to see something," I pacified them by promising to give some manifestations at the next lecture. I was then allowed to proceed. The receipts of the lecture I had undertaken to give to the Workmen's Hall, a young institution in need of funds, but a letter appearing in a local journal, virtually declining the money, I decided on appropriating it to another and perhaps better purpose. The committee of the institution in question, I afterwards learned, had authorised the letter to be written in deference to the views of the founder (described in to-day's Gazette, as one of Nature's noblemen), who regarded the proceeds of my lecture in the light of "Devil's money!"

A day or two after this I was in communication with the spirit-world, and said to my principal communicant. "Do you see the great men who have lived on the earth?"

Yes.

" Have you seen Shakespeare,"

No.

" Have you seen Mendelsshon?',

No.

" Have you seen Prince Albert?"

Yes, frequently.

"Could you bring him here?"

I will try.

The next day I enquired as to the probability of a visit from Prince Albert, and was informed he had consented to come and would be present at half-past eleven the following morning. We accordingly assembled at the appointed time, and were at once in communication with our spirit-friends, who said,

Prince Albert is coming in five minutes, so be ready for him.

I said, we will sing his Christmas hymn. I may observe that we were in the habit of having music at our *Séances*, which we found greatly to facilitate the manifestations. So, on the Prince being announced, we commenced the hymn alluded to, and he at once began to beat time with a stick which was resting against a wall beside the harmonium.

The hymn finished, the Prince wrote these words.

It is very kind of you all to learn it to sing to me; you did it very nicely indeed. Albert of Saxe-Coburgh and Gotha died at Windsor Castle in 1861.

At the conclusion of this writing, the large dining-room table, at which my daughter, the (medium) was sitting, was raised at one end. This was a phenomenon I had never before witnessed through my daughter's mediumship. In this case the table was covered with a cloth and not a hand had touched it. I have since seen this table, which weighs about a hundred-weight, raised in the air by spirit power. I next proposed some more singing, and observed that I had composed a Christmas hymn. The Prince asked us to sing it but wished his own to be sung again first. This request was complied with, and on the completion of my hymn, the words *It is worthy* were written. We then sang a piece from Mozart, which happened to be on the instrument, to which the Prince beat the time with the ability of a Costa. I then asked "Are you often with the Queen?"

Yes, very often.

"Are you pleased at the birth of a Prince?" at which great delight was manifested.

After a few remarks concerning Spiritualism, in which the Prince expressed himself greatly interested, and which he said, would be pretty generally believed in five years, the interview terminated. I need not say that it afforded us all great gratification. At a *Séance* the following day, allusion was made to these proceedings, and the words "We were very pleased he came to see you," were rapped out.

D

CHAPTER V.

*Manifestations in public—The facts are published—
Diversity of opinions prevail—Nangle of Skreen—
Vigilans—Golden harps in Heaven—The Hail-
sham Ghost.*

My second lecture came off a fortnight after the
first, when there being no Molly Downing to draw a
promiscuous crowd, the noisy element was absent.
I was consequently listened to much more attentively than before, and a good deal of interest
appeared to be manifested in the subject.   At the
close of the lecture, according to my promise, I
made some experiments with a table which moved
and banged about in a very violent manner.   I
left the platform and took my seat among the audience.   My position was in the second or third
row ; at any rate I was at least 16 feet from the
table.   Holding an alphabet in my hand I pointed
to the letters, which was witnessed by the gentlemen sitting on either side of me ; and one of them
wrote the letters down as they were indicated by
the knocking of the table.   Several persons having mounted the platform the table was nearly
obscured from view, so that I had to go entirely
by the sound.   After knocking at about forty

letters the table became quiet. "Is that all?" I asked. Three knocks in reply. I then said to the gentleman who had taken down the letters "Will you have the kindness to read the sentence." I had been too much engaged in pointing to the alphabet to take cognizance of the words as they were formed, and at the conclusion had no idea what the sentence was. It was this:— *You must all believe in Spiritualism for the truth will come out*; and truly a very appropriate one for the occasion.

Here then was another wonderful fact. It is obvious that there must have been some connection between the table and the alphabet—some invisible telegraph, otherwise an intelligent sentence could not have been obtained in the way it was. The power that moved the table must at the same time have seen the alphabet I held in my hand. I leave my readers to judge whether any but the spiritual theory will account for a fact of this kind. It is of no use saying it is electricity or some such blind force. Electricity may be the medium of conveying intelligence, as in telegraphy, but it is not, and cannot be, the source of intelligence. Notices of my lectures appearing, not only in the local but in the county papers, gave additional notoriety to the subject, and a knowledge of it was no longer confined to Eastbourne but spread throughout the county. The Brighton papers also took up the theme, and it was pretty generally canvassed by the inhabitants of the "Little London by the Sea." In addition to the articles my lectures had called forth, letters were published against Spiritualism which served also to give it greater publicity. In these letters all classes of opponents appeared to be represented.

There was the scientific materialist with his challenge, and the orthodox religionist with his devil-theory. One writer descanted very learnedly on the operation of unknown natural forces, and whilst admitting the reality of the phenomena, attributed the intelligence displayed in them to the minds of the operators. Another, evidently some country rector who probably was in the habit of regarding his parish as the whole world, or at least the most important part of it, wrote in a brief and authoritative manner saying, "it was high time it was put a stop to—it had gone quite far enough!" To show the absurd nature of the opposition that was manifested, I give the particulars of the challenge before alluded to. They are as follow. That the challenger and myself should each deposit fifty pounds—that a table should be placed in an open field—that I was not to go near till the time of trial, and then not nearer than 15 feet. If under, these conditions the table rose 30 feet in the air, I was to be entitled to the £50, and if it did not the challenger was to have the money. The gentleman who made this preposterous challenge is now, I believe, a convert to Spiritualism.

The letter of the orthodox clergyman signing himself ",Vigilans" who sought to throw the onus on Beelzebub, was mainly an extract from the book of the Rev. E. Nangle, an Irish priest, immortalized by Mr. Howitt in some lines commencing,

> "Nangle of Skreen, what does he mean?
> That the Devil's converted, or turned very green.
> The Pamphlet he gives us is not vastly new,
> It only takes up the old cry of the Jew,
> Who said, when he saw our Lord healing the sick,
> 'Oh! that is the work of that crafty Old Nick.'"

In this letter (a column and a half of small type) it was related how a clergyman got into communication with a spirit, evidently not a first-class one, who gave in reply to his questions just what was looked for, and ended the conference by assuring him he was the Devil himself, which the said clergyman of course believed. It was a foregone conclusion with him, and on this peg hung the whole argument.

A curious circumstance occured about this time in reference to the writer of this letter, at least I have always identified "Vigilans" with one of our local clergy. This gentleman conceived it to be his duty to call on me to warn me against Spiritualism. I told him I could find nothing objectionable in it ; that all the communications I received were of an excellent and satisfactory character, particularly those addressed to my children, which were pervaded by a highly religious spirit and produced in them a good and salutary effect. I repeated some of them to him, of which the following are specimens.

My dear niece, you must follow the holy precepts, and counsels of Jesus, darling child. I am your guardian angel. Look towards Heaven as your safeguard. Never forget. Do what I tell you.

Kate is here and she loves you very much. When you go to bed pray to God.

Mary, I hope you try to love God and that you make a happy home for your dear papa and brothers and sister.

Heaven is a very beautiful place ; we sing lovely songs and play on golden harps.

Such are some of the spirit-messages I submitted to this worthy clergyman, who was forced to admit their unexceptional character. He left

me and went straight to Mr. Hicks to warn him also
against Spiritualism.   Mr. Hicks like myself referred to the messages we received in proof that
there was nothing bad in it.   " Yes " said the
clergyman, "Mr. Cooper has shewn me some of
them; there was one about playing golden harps
in heaven; now I would as soon believe there are
tables and chairs in heaven as golden harps."
After some conversation, which was no more avail-
ing in altering the opinion of Mr. Hicks than my
own, " Vigilans "left.   The next day was Sunday
and after breakfast our spirit friends made their
presence known as they were in the habit of doing
at this time, and I asked them to make a communication.

Not now, we will come again at half-past twelve,—
was the answer by raps.   We met at the appointed time and almost immediately there was
written in the middle of a sheet of note paper

There are golden harps in heaven,
and in the left-hand corner

For Mr.————.
The hand-writing was that of my wife, and,
taking one of her original letters from a desk, I
sent it and the message to the clergyman to whom
it was addressed.

Encouraged by the success of my lectures in
Eastbourne, I determined on repeating them in
the neighbouring towns.   The first I visited was
Hailsham, about eight miles distant, where my
lecture was well attended and listened to with interest.   The M. D. of the town, however, who was
present, manifested his displeasure by abruptly
quitting the room when I was about half-way
through.

I was, at the time, reading a case of haunting from Robert Dale Owen's book. These he pronounced 'Joe Millerisms,' and said it was an insult to common sense to talk about such things in the present day. At the close of the lecture a demand was made to "see something" and I then found that the people here, as at Eastbourne, had come under the impression that they would witness some of the extraordinary things they had heard of. With some little dissatisfaction expressed on this head the proceedings terminated. The following week I paid another visit to Hailsham which was attended with very unexpected results. Owing to the absence of manifestations my lecture was not sufficiently attractive to draw an audience on the second occasion. The time for commencement had considerably passed, and not more than a score of persons were present. I was conversing with some of them when the "Hailsham Ghost" put in an appearance, causing consternation on all hands; even the sceptics turned white and looked dismayed. The particulars of this affair will be gathered from the following letters which appeared in the county paper, Mr. "Hard of Belief" being none other than the M.D. who thought it beneath his dignity to sit my lecture out. It may be well, however, to explain before giving the letters, that while we were talking at one end of the room, suddenly, underneath the platform at the other end, a succession of heavy reports were heard, causing the table to tremble and the dust to rise. An examination was made under the platform by those who had sufficient courage to advance in the direction of the mysterious sounds, but nothing could be found to account for them, and the mystery was increased when it was found there was no cellar under the room. After sundry vain attempts at an explanation the company dispersed, and the next day being market day (the market was held in this very room), the affair became the chief theme of conversation and almost superseded all other matters. The bucolic mind went away wonder-struck—the people carried the news to their respective homes, and doubtless made a greater impression in favour of Spiritualism than my lecture would have produced even if delivered to a well-filled hall. Although the affair was never properly cleared up, I have no doubt it was the trick of some wag, who intended the noises to take place under my feet while I was lecturing, but was defeated in this by the lecture not beginning at the appointed time. This is the correspondence that ensued :—

The Hailsham Ghost.

Sir,—In common with all the world, we in this quiet little town of Hailsham, had heard of the wonderful doings by Mr. Cooper, of Eastbourne—as who has not? of his holding daily, nay hourly communication with the shades of the departed—of the good advice given by these spirits to their former companions in this "vale of tears," how they were to be good boys and girls—get their lessons properly, &c. We had been informed, too, that the Eastbourners walked about the streets in fear and trembling, lest some of those returned spirits would disclose secrets and peccadilloes, which were never meant to "come to light," and we heard how many dreaded to be out after dark, for fear of meeting "Molly Downing" deceased some months since, whom many averred to have seen walking the Parade "just as she used to do." Well, Mr. Editor, we had heard all these wonderful things, and many of us held our breath in amazement, and we whispered to each other " can such things be, and not overcome us with special wonder," but just imagine our excitement when we read from bills in our shop windows that Mr. Cooper intended giving a lecture in our Corn Exchange, on " Spiritual manifestations." Now, sir, I beg to assure you that though we are generally a quiet and sober people, a few of us must plead guilty to occasionally having " some spiritual manifestations," particularly after passing a pleasant evening with our friends. Still curiosity compelled us to witness some of Cooper's " Manifestations," as we fancied they might be different to those of our experience. Consequently a goodly company assembled at the hour appointed for the lecture, and gave an attentive hearing to all he had to say, in the shape of stories of dreams, apparitions, &c., and at which most of us laughed, as we detected that many of them were collected from that respectable authority, " Joe Miller," and others owing their existence to that no less respectable author, " Mr. Penny-a-line ;" after a while we became tired of these stories and requested a display of these *manifestations* so much talked about, but to our dismay we were informed that it could not be done that evening as he had not brought his "medium" with him. So some of us became rather excited, thinking we had been done out of our money, and I fancy the *hirsute money-taker* would have been handled rather roughly had we not been appeased by a promise to come again shortly, and bring the "medium" with him. Well, sir, according to promise he "showed out" last evening. Warned by former experience, not more than a dozen of us attended ; one came four miles, paid his sixpence, and loudly demanded to see his old master, our late respected friend and neighbour, Mr. King Sampson. He declared he must either see him, or have his sixpence back ; the latter very reasonable demand was, I believe, eventually complied with, and now in great and wonderful expectation we accompany Cooper and his *double* to the scene room ; but scarcely had he put his foot within the doorway when *bang, bang*, rings through the room—a noise sufficient to wake the dead. " What noise is that ? " cries Cooper, rather in dismay ; audience gaped and stared, horror struck. Hirsute *money-taker* exclaims—

" *Powerful manifestations ;*" " *ow hever can you now disbelieve such hexemplifications ; you require hevidence of han hearthquake.*"

Knock, knock, bang, bang, goes the ghost in the very centre of the room. Cooper tries to advance to the chair, but no. *Bang, bang,* goes the ghost, and stops him. Pale and trembling he asks, " Is there any cellar under this room ?" " No," there is no cellar. *Bang, bang,* again goes the ghost ; no little tap, tap, nor even the loud sharp postman's rap, rap, but great and powerful strokes, as if given with a sledge-hammer—consternation reigns around. " Bless us, what can it be ?" cry some ; others cry "Search the room," so some of the boldest look under the tables, chairs, into the crevices, and up the chimney, and, indeed, I observed one taking a cautious squint into an ink-stand. But nothing satisfactory is discovered ; still *bang, bang,* goes the ghost, search round the walls, nothing to be noted there, out rushes *money-taker,* and timourously asks the landlord if " his 'ouse is subject to noises ?" " Oh, yes," landlord replies, " very often indeed, especially when there is a jolly party dining here." *Thump, thump, bang, bang,* goes the ghost again. Now all is consternation—some declare the devil is under the floor. How could he get there ? why a mouse or a fly could scarcely get through the air grating ; still more than ever goes the ghost, and one of our most respectable cordwainers, feeling very nervous, leaves the room, declaring that he saw the ghost ascend through the floor as high as the ceiling, in the shape of a cloud of dust, through which a poor girl plainly saw the table jump up, and the two candles glare at her so maliciously that she bolted home, and so frightened the household there that there was no sleep for them that night. *Bang, bang*, still goes the ghost, and Cooper and his hirsute *money-taker*, in fear and dismay rush from the room, leaving very few, you may be sure behind them, to the front bar, where they receive the *commiseration and sympathy* of the friends assembled there, who kindly hoped they would get home safely, but said it would take a good sum to induce them to accompany them even as far as Polegate. The cry now became " Let us get home," and off they ran to the station to catch the last train ; and the *roars of laughter* that followed them, would have cured any case of rheumatics, and we hope will be a " caution " to all *spirit rappers* in future.

Now Mr. Editor, if you, or any of your friends, wish to see a real ghost,—none of your old fashioned, spectre-looking things, dressed in a long winding-sheet, pale and wan, and gliding past you with a noiseless tread ; no, no, not that sort of a ghost at all, but a real modern one ; a good thumping ghost, one that can make you feel and hear him too.—come to the Crown Inn at Hailsham, and there you will have your curiosity gratified, and the worthy landlord will do his best to allay your fears and your thirst at the same time, by exhibiting to you the ghost in the shape of two or three *clothes props*, bound together, and truly terrific monsters they are. So now, Mr. Editor, having told you all our experiences of " Spiritual Manifestations," and feeling a little tired, I will end by hoping neither you nor I will ever get a "rap" from the Hailsham ghost.

ONE HARD OF BELIEF.

February, 1864.

Reappearance of the Hailsham Ghost.

Sir,—The Hailsham news in your last week's paper is of a very *unique* character, being made up of two items—an extraordinary litter of pups, and an extraordinary litter of lies. It was my intention not to

have noticed the production of one "Hard of Belief,"
who has thought fit to air his wit at the expense of the
Spiritualists, for I considered the public would have
looked upon it as I did, as a clever squib exploded to
create fun, at which, perhaps, no one laughed more
heartily than myself.   If it did not cure rheumatics,
it, at any rate, dispelled a fit of indigestion.   Finding,
however, that persons really believe the account, and
are desiring to know whether my nervous system has
recovered the shock, and are moreover apprehensive
that the occurrence may hasten the fulfilment of the
predictions (notwithstanding the consolation you
kindly tendered me) of my being at Hayward's Heath
before long, I desire to give a brief account of what
took place on the occasion alluded to.

At a former lecture, which was merely introduc-
tory to the one proposed to be given, some dissatisfaction was evinced on account of no (H)ocular demon-
stration being afforded.   The consequence was, on the
second occasion, the audience did not muster very
strong at first, and those who did come were not a
class of persons I cared to lecture to, They wanted
something "sensational."   I therefore directed the
money to be returned, and waited the arrival of train
time.   After a little while the numbers increased to
above thirty, and a desire was expressed for the lecture
to be given.   At this time I was engaged in telling a
little knot of the " Hard of Belief" fraternity, how a
doctor in this county had his scepticism put to flight
by witnessing the destruction of a large table by
spiritual power in his own house, when some noises
were heard at the other end of the room, which really
I took but little notice of, imagining them to be made to
frighten a drunken man, who was making vociferous
demands to see the devil.   After a short interval the
noises were repeated, and a search was made to discover their cause.   No one, however, was found under
the platform, nor up the chimney, both of which
places were well examined.   I did not observe the individual "squinting into the inkstand," but I will not

say no one did so, for the Hailsham people, as is well known, are shrewd investigators. An enquiry was next made of the landlord, and on his reporting that it was not possible for the noises to be made underneath the room, the astonishment increased, and assumed an air of mystery, and I could not help remarking that those who had been the loudest in avowing their "hardness of belief," were, of all others, the most pale-faced and panic-stricken, thus verifying what Dr. Johnson says, that "they who deny it by their tongues confess it by their fears." As for myself I have had too much to do with real ghosts lately to be frightened by ghosts made up of a few clothes props.

My own impression is, that Mr. "Hard of Belief's" point of view was from the snug little bar parlor, where, under spirituous influence, and through the medium of tobacco-smoke, he witnessed the powerful manifestations he describes, saw the glare of the two candles that had not been lighted, heard five volleys of "bangs" that did not go off, and conceived the rest of his wonderful story, which would not discredit the most practised "penny-a-liner." The letter only required one ingredient, viz., truth, to make it a first-rate affair, but wanting that, it is merely a weak invention of the enemy, affording an illustration, how in a weak cause, persons are compelled to resort to persecution, ridicule, and such like forms of opposition, instead of reasoning and legitimate argumentation.

I remain, yours, &c.

ROBERT COOPER.

Eastbourne, February, 20th, 1864.

CHAPTER VI.

Spiritualism at Lewes — Manifestations of Bigotry and Rowdyism—Sparrows—Squibs and Crackers— Personal danger—In the dark—Escape.

Nothing daunted by the "Hailsham Ghost," after lecturing at Windmill Hill, a small town close by, I announced a lecture at the county town of Lewes, a hotbed of religious bigotry and intolerance, where the various isms from ritualism to quakerism thrive most flourishingly. At the appointed hour a goodly number of persons had assembled at the Corn Exchange, many of whom were of the upper classes of the town. There was nothing whatever at the commencement of the lecture to indicate the warm reception that was provided for me; and it was not till I had proceeded with it for nearly half-an-hour, that any symptoms of disorder were manifested. The first mutterings of the storm were caused by one of the forms in the rear being thrown down occasionally, producing a sound that reverberated through the spacious hall, and drowning for the time my voice. This I, at first, supposed to be accidental, but as it continued I appealed to the audience to be quiet for the sake of those who might wish to hear what I had to say. Then the *fracas* began in earnest; sparrows were let loose in order to divert attention, and squibs and crackers were discharged in the room to the great terror of the ladies, one of whose dresses narrowly escaped being ignited, and she left the room in consequence. Order being somewhat restored I continued my lecture and began to think I should get through it after all, but some remarks I made, not suiting the narrow views of the religionists in the front seats, caused the proceedings to take a new and unexpected turn. The remarks I made that gave such offence will be found further on; they appeared to me plain and simple statements and of a perfectly unobjectionable character. One gentleman, however, was of a different opinion. He rose from his seat and with great warmth said, he "would not sit there to hear all religion blasphemed," and abruptly left the room, and was followed by others; whilst those who remained, principally the occupants of the back seats, rushed towards the platform and surrounded me; and, under the pretext that they had not seen any manifestations, demanded back their money. They then showed signs of molestation; throwing the water that stood on the table over me and pushing me off the platform. Mr. Powell, who had come forward, received a share of the same kind of treatment. At length a few gentlemen who had some influence with the mob —for it is worthy no better designation—remonstrated with them and advised me to leave the room, but this I refused to do, although they seemed to "mean mischief." The number of malcontents gradually became less, and on the light being extinguished my protectors escorted

me safely to the hotel. I consider myself mainly
indebted to these gentlemen for my escape from
the jaws of the lion. I afterwards learned that an
attempt was made to extinguish the gas in the
midst of my lecture, but the man who had
the key, valued his place too much to accept the
consideration offered him, to give it to those who
wished to obtain it. Hence the contemplated
dark *Séance* which would, in all probability, have
been attended with powerful manifestations did
not take place. Here is an account of the affair
from the *Sussex Express*, also a letter of mine containing the remarks that caused the indignation
that was manifested, and led to the abrupt termination of the meeting.

Spiritualism at the Corn Exchange.

On Wednesday evening last Mr. R. Cooper, of Eastbourne, addressed a numerous assembly at the Corn
Exchange, on "Modern Spirit Manifestations."
Having requested an Englishman's privilege of being
heard patiently until the close of the lecture, when he
would invite discussion, Mr. Cooper proceeded to say
that some might ridicule the subject, as he had done
himself formerly. Indeed, if any one had told him six
or seven months ago that he would ultimately believe
in spiritual manifestations, he would have flatly contradicted them, but Spiritualism was brought before
his notice, and he investigated it at first from curiosity,
and after a careful study of the question he came to
the conclusion that it was what it professed to be —
truth (oh, oh, and ironical cheers). He set out with
this proposition, "Let me have one fact clearly established, however trivial, out of the ordinary course of

nature, and I shall be prepared to think everything I have heard may have been, and possibly was, true." Now, he had seen not only one fact, but hundreds, out of the ordinary course of nature ; for instance, he had seen a large and heavy table, without castors, move about the room in his own house ; and if that was not out of the ordinary course of nature, he hoped the learned Editor who had been holding him up to ridicule at Eastbourne lately would come forward and explain it (laughter and cheers.) Mr. Faraday had attempted to explain it, but had failed to do so, and had played a part in a farce as broad as any ever put on the boards of the Adelphi (laughter and counter cheers), and he (Mr. Cooper) thought that his judgment upon the matter was quite as good as Mr. Faraday's, or any other man's (laughter). The subject was of great interest to all, for who would deny that there was a natural instinct which taught us to look beyond the tomb, and to endeavour to gain an insight into that state on which they must all sooner or later enter. All religion in the world recognised the communion of the people inhabiting the earth with seen and unseen spirits, and this was true of Christianity. Having mentioned several instances in the New Testament, in which spirits had appeared to living men and women, which were not always angels, because Moses and Elias were seen, Mr. Cooper went on to state that spiritual influences were believed in by some of the greatest men who ever lived, by Socrates, Cicero, Pope, Dryden, Milton, Dr. Johnson, Byron, &c. Dreams in modern times were generally held to be utterly meaningless, but unquestionably the ancients believed in their prophetic character. In this country, however, the importance of dreams had been proved again and again. He instanced the murder of Maria Martin, some forty years ago. She was killed by a man she was connected with named Corder, but his guilt was not discovered, till her mother three times successively dreamed that the body of her daughter was buried in an adjoining barn. There it was found, and

E

in the end the man was hanged. Mr. Cooper then alluded to unaccountable noises heard in houses, which
he attributed to the doings of spirits, and related
several anecdotes of the pranks these supernatural
visitors played. Some years ago loud and extraordi-
narily strange noises took place in a gentleman's house,
and continued for a long time ; they were so loud as
to be heard in the adjoining village, and this was tes-
tified to by the late John Wesley, on whose veracity
many of them could rely (cheers). Belief in apparitions had been ascribed to nervousness, but how was it
then that they had shuddered when exposed to supernatural influences. (A dismal howl from some "dog"
in the back-ground and considerable laughter). The
extraordinary freaks of the spirits at the haunted house
at Romney Marsh, which were next referred to, were
fully reported in our paper at the time ; the furniture
of the house jumped about in a most amusing and
singular, not to say alarming manner. The tables and
chairs danced round the room ; some boots on the
floor flew up to the ceiling and alighted on the table ;
the crockery ware kept time with the tables and chairs
and rattled away. Bedsteads marched gravely down-
stairs. A Bible left its place on the drawers in the
bedroom, ran down stairs, and hit a little girl on the
shoulder. Mr. Cooper stated that he actually proceeded to the locality, and the circumstances were
verified to him by a young man, who had seen much
of it himself. The lecturer then proceeded to the real
point of the whole affair,—the question of mediums.
The best were generally females. It might be asked
what constituted a "medium?" and he would answer
the question by asking another, "How is it that one
man's nose is longer than another?" (laughter)—that
one man could see further, and another hear better
than others. So it was with respect to spiritual manifestations. One person had greater capacity for holding spiritual communication than another, and where
that faculty was developed in an extraordinary degree
they had a first-rate medium. Apparitions were often

ascribed to a disordered stomach or an overtasked brain, but what became of those suppositions when they had to account for apparitions which were observed by more than one person at the same time. Surely every one must conclude that this was not imaginary. (At this juncture a number of live sparrows were let loose from the body of the exchange, they flew towards the platform, amidst some laughter and cries of " Look out, there are some spirits for you.") The lecturer, however, continued, the audience generally remaining attentive, that theologians held that spirits after death could not return to earth, and therefore, could not communicate with its inhabitants. He would tell them a few instances. When the celebrated Miss Porter was living at Esher, in Surrey, an old gentleman in the village used frequently to visit her of an afternoon for the purpose of reading a newspaper and partaking of a cup of tea. One evening he came in and seated himself ; she addressed an observation to him, but receiving no reply, looked up, and saw that he was gone ; thinking he was ill, and gone home, she sent to enquire after him, and the answer was that the gentleman had died an hour before. He would also give them two examples which had come to his knowledge at Eastbourne. There was a poor woman living at Eastbourne, named Pierson, who gained a livelihood by washing and charring ; her husband had been a soldier in the Peninsular War, and at Waterloo, and was at this time an invalid in bed with the rheumatism. On one occasion Mrs. Pierson went out to wash, &c., at a Mrs. Griffin's ; and while she was down on her knees scrubbing the floor, she looked up and saw her husband standing near her in his shirt, and to show the prejudice of people, he might state that a Hastings paper had accused him of indecency in talking of a spirit in a shirt (laughter). To proceed with the anecdote, Mrs. Pierson advanced towards the apparition, which disappeared at once. When Mrs. Griffin came down she told her it was her fancy, but when the poor woman got home, sad to say, she found her husband dead on the floor, he having broken a blood vessel. Another instance was, that formerly an old woman, named Downing, kept a sweet shop, and under cover of this, used to sell contraband spirits to the sailors. Her house was, some time after her death, occupied by a Mr. Cook, and one morning last year he awoke about a quarter past five and saw her apparition in his room. A fisherman named Hide, passing the house early one morning, also saw the apparition. She appeared to be about fifteen yards from him. He halloed to his sons, but receiving no answer walked towards her ; as he advanced the apparition receded and turned side-face to ,him, and a very luminous halo rendered her face and figure very distinct; she then vanished. A woman named Kught also saw her. The lecturer, having thus prepared the way, by a variety of marvellous statements, all resting on totally insufficient evidence, as any man, with a reasoning power would have told Mr. Cooper, proceeded to raise, as he said, his superstructure, that is to dilate on the wonders and progress of Spiritualism in this country and generally. The audience had, however, from the first consisted of two classes ; one bent on hearing the lecture, the other on having a spree, in imitation of the Hailsham affair. The latter were in the back seats, and those had gradually increased. So one of the benches which had fallen with a loud noise at intervals was now plied with great vigour. Then crackers were let off in the room, and at this stage the respectable part of the audience began to disappear. The lecturer most injudiciously, too, assailed the audience who might have been " managed " by one more adroit, but the final blow was given by a monstrous and utterly uncalled for onslaught on Christianity. He had already ventured on the assertion that the evidence on which the wonders of spiritualist *Séances* rested was stronger than that of the miracles in the New Testament, the one being matter of recorded, and the other of *rira roce*, testimony. Then he went on to say that the dispensation of Judaism had lasted 4,000 years ; that of Christianity 2,000 years ; and now, to give faith in the soul's immortality, belief in which had ceased to be real, the dispensation of Spiritualism was—when Mr. Macrae rose, and declaring that he could no longer remain to hear all religion assailed, left the room. He was followed by Mr. Button, who, however, returned, and many others, and after this there being a slight lull, the lecturer proceeded more in dumb show, however, than anything else. The form fell incessantly, and at last Mr. Powell went on the platform, and a consultation took place. A little knot of the auditory gathered round, and then we found Mr. Bates cross-examining Mr. Cooper with respect to a bag of nuts, the number in which the spirits at some previous lecture elsewhere, had failed to state accurately. There was great excitement in the room, and Mr. Cooper being in positive, personal danger, Mr. R. Crosskey appealed to the party with some success, to leave the room in peace. Gradually the numbers present had lessened ; the stalwart form of Mr. Geer, of the Star Hotel, was seen looming in the distance, and a couple of policemen became distinctly visible. So, though there was still evidently some danger of " a rush " at Mr. Cooper when he got off the platform, none took place, and even when the last light was extinguished, Mr. Cooper passed safely through the room and secured an undisturbed retreat to the interior of the hotel. Of course, Mr. Powell accompanied him. It is quite absurd in any one to attempt to give " lectures " on Spiritualism unaccompanied by a medium.

In explanation of the matter which had given offence to a portion of the audience, I wrote the following letter to the Editor of the *Sussex Express* :— .

SIR,—In justice to myself and the cause I have at
heart, I wish to lay before the public the precise words
which gave such great offence at my lecture at Lewes.
After showing that Spiritualism was calculated to act
as a powerful agent in promoting Christian truth, I
said, "Some think the Bible is sufficient,—that it is
the sole and sufficient rule of faith and practice,—that
it contains everything necessary for man's salvation. '

"Such is doubtless the case as far as those who believe in it are concerned. But what of the millions
upon millions all over the continent, especially in Germany, France, and Spain, to say nothing of vast numbers in our own country, who are the most confirmed
and positive materialists, rejecting Christianity, and
for the most part a God. If such be the case after near
2,000 years of Christianity, and above 4,000 years of
Judaism, it clearly proves some new dispensation to be
necessary to bring home to the mind of man the fact
of his immortality and his accountability. We have
it on the authority of Professor Hare, that in his time
25,000 atheists and deists, in America alone, had been
converted by Spiritualism to Christianity.'

Such is the statement I made, and still make, and I
challenge any one to controvert it.

The remarks I made on the superiority of personal
evidence over historical testimony, is a proposition so
self-evident, that I cannot imagine any but the most
narrow-minded and shallow-pated bigot, whose ideas
are circumscribed by the four walls of his conventicle,
gainsaying it.

I remain, &c.

ROBERT COOPER..

Eastbourne, March, 5th, 1864.

To which the Editor appended the following
note—

[Mr. Cooper has repeated in substance the remarks which aroused the indignation of the Lewes meeting. We cannot allow our columns to be made the vehicle of sentiments which can only arouse the unanimous indignation of our readers. What the Rev. Mr. Nangle would say to Spiritualism as developed by Mr. Cooper, it seems difficult to determine.]

———————

CHAPTER VII.

Another Lecture—A Noble Chairman— Correspon-
dence— A mare's-nest — Spirit-messages—Curious
experiences—A nocturnal visit.

The next day I visited Uckfield, a small inland
town about eight miles from Lewes. The first
thing that greeted my eye on arriving there was
a display of large posters, stuck side by side, occupying several square feet of the wall. The most
prominent words on these bills were "Attend,"
and "Spiritualism," and I at first thought they
were put up in my interest, but on closer examination I found they contained texts from the Old
Testament against witchcraft, and were evidently
the work of an opponent. I was afterwards informed they were stuck up by order of the resident
clergyman. The room, in spite of the unfavourable state of the weather, was well filled at the
time appointed for the lecture to begin. At my
request a gentleman was appointed by the meeting to the chair. I did not know him at the time
but was afterwards informed it was Captain Noble,
who resided in the neighbourhood and filled the
office of county magistrate. He commenced by de-

precating the conduct of the Lewes people, remarking "that any fool could make a noise but it wanted a wise man to use an argument." He also expressed his disapproval of the clergyman's proceedings in reference to the bills that were placarded about the town. The chairman's judicious remarks produced their intended effect, and my lecture passed off without interruption. I was listened to with considerable attention and great interest was evidently felt in the subject. At the conclusion Captain Noble got up, and, after stating that he had studied scientific subjects for many years, proceeded to raise the usual objections that are advanced by this class of objectors, advancing the Stockwell and Cock Lane Ghosts in proof of the fallacy of all supernatural occurrences. He also raised the objection generally raised by scientific men in reference to the dress of apparitions, ridiculing the idea of the "Ghost of clothes." In a few days a letter appeared in the "Sussex Advertiser" relative to my lecture, which resulted in a published correspondence between myself and Captain Noble, in which the noble chairman displayed great ability and acumen, so much so, that a gentleman of high position in London wrote to caution me, saying that I had no mean antagonist to deal with. In the course of the correspondence Captain Noble overstepped the bounds of propriety, and, possibly, legality, by calling Mr. Home a rank impostor. For this, he was called to account, and threatened with an action for libel, but on his making a gentlemanly and honorable apology, no further steps were taken in the matter. After this I visited Hastings, and thus ended my first series of lectures ; and I had then no idea of giving any more.

Spiritualism at Uckfield.

" I have studied this subject, and practically examined it
these seven years, and I know much cleverer men who have
done this much longer."—WILLIAM HOWITT.

SIR,—" Go it ye cripples, crutches are cheap," is an
old saying, revived by Professor De Morgan, as applic-
able to the opponents of Spiritualism, and appears to
me to be particularly suited to the Uckfieldites. who,
failing to provide anything in the shape of a Hailsham
ghost, or Lewes crackers, find fault with my lecture,
not with anything I advanced, but on account of the
absence of the " sensational." Well, I will do my
Uckfield audience the compliment to say that on no
occasion, except at Hastings, have I been listened to
with such respectful and interested attention as on
last Thursday week. If I could only have caused a
table to dance about a little, the lecture would have
been a triumph in every respect. At the conclusion,
the chairman, in a very gentlemanly and proper manner, advanced some objections which I imagined to have
been satisfactorily replied to at the time, but such not
being the case, I ask you to grant me a little space to
set the matter in a right light before the public.

In the course of my lecture I alluded to two or
three supernatural events of historic note. One was
the well-known case of the drummer of Tedworth, and
another the extraordinary and equally well-known
affair that occurred in the family of the celebrated
John Wesley. Captain Noble accused me of forgetting to tell the audience what a certain Mrs. Cleaver
(is she any relation of Mrs. Partington, and like her
thinks to keep back the sea of Spiritualism with a
broom ?) had said on the subject. I preferred relying
on higher authorities than Mrs. Cleaver or Clever (I
don't know how the name is spelt), and I find, in reference to the Tedworth affair, that the following is a
compendium of the essential facts in the case, literally

extracted from the Rev. Joseph Glanvil's account. who was chaplain to Charles II.: —

The disturbances continued for two entire years - namely, from April, 1661, until April, 1663 ; and Mr. Mompesson took up his quarters for the night, for two months at a time, in a particular chamber, expressly for the purpose of observing them. The sounds produced were so loud as to awaken the neighbours in the adjoining village, at a considerable distance from Mr. Mompessons's house. The motion in the children's bed in Mr. Glanvil's presence, was so great as to shake the doors and windows of the house. The facts collected by Glanvil at the time they occurred, were published by him four years afterwards, to wit 1666, and the more important of these facts were sworn to in a court of justice. And ten years after these occurrences took place, and when it was reported that Mr. Mompesson had admitted the discovery of a trick, that gentleman explicitly denied that he had ever discovered any natural cause for the phenomena, and in the most solemn manner indorsed his former declarations to Mr. Glanvil.

Again, with reference to the occurrences in the Wesley family, we have the testimony of John Wesley himself, and other members of the family, and an account was also published by the philosopher Priestly, fully admitting the facts. The events in question lasted two months, and John Wesley made a special journey to his father's house for the purpose of witnessing them ; and with reference to the Romney Marsh affair I had the testimony of the inmates of the two houses, and a young farmer, who happened to be present when I was there, described several extraordinary circumstances that he had witnessed. It was, however, with great difficulty that I could induce old Mrs. Gates to tell me anything about it. With streaming eyes she said she wished to forget it.

I was also reminded that I had forgotten to allude to the Cock-Lane Ghost, an account of which was then given, but in doing so the gentleman neglected to

observe that " The girl was removed from one place
to another, and was said to be constantly attended
with the usual noises, though bound and muffled hand
and foot, and that without any motion in her lips, and
when she appeared to be asleep ; nay, they were
often said to be heard in rooms at a considerable distance from that where she lay." The noises at length
ceased, and on being told that her father and mother
would be sent to Newgate if she did not reproduce
them, she took a piece of board to bed with her and
began knocking and scratching upon it, and it was at
once remarked that " these noises were not like those
which used to be made." This, however, was given
forth as the explanation of the mystery which had
" excited the interest of the learned and the unlearned,
the high and the low, the rich and the poor, the noble
and the beggar, and for months was almost the only
topic of conversation, not merely in the metropolis but
throughout the whole kingdom."

The chairman also took exception to the apparitions
of Mrs. Downing and Allen Pierson, on the ground
that they appeared dressed ; consequently he argued
there must be the ghosts of clothes. It would certainly, to my mind, have been very improper for
them to appear without attire. The evidence on which
these alleged appearances rest I fully stated. The
witnesses are known to me, and I believe are all
trustworthy. But it is with the objection raised that
I would say a few words.

The objection, it will be seen, is of wide range. It
applies not only to the well-attested accounts of ghosts
in secular history, in all ages, as well as contemporary
records, but also to those of the Scriptures. Samuel,
when called up by the Witch of Endor, came
" wrapped in a mantle ;" of the angel who rolled back
the stone from the door of the sepulchre, we are told
that his " raiment" was " white as snow." We are
told that when Mary saw the risen Saviour she " knew
not that it was Jesus," but supposed him to be the
gardener. He must therefore have appeared clothed

like ordinary humanity. The angel who appeared to Daniel appeared as a man, "clothed in linen," and so on. Now I do not mean to assert that the worthy chairman has intentionally sought to cast ridicule upon these narratives, but the fact that he has thus, however unconsciously, supplied material for ribald jesting to the sceptic and scorner of holy writ, will, I hope, make him pause, and reconsider the propriety of burlesquing a subject, capable, at least in other hands of this application, and to reflect that, perhaps, he may have made a mistake, and that the Bible and universal experience after all are right. At any rate his objection appears to me quite as censurable as my asserting that I esteem that which I see with my own eyes and feel with my own hands, superior testimony to that I read of having taken place eighteen centuries ago.

Exception was also taken to Miss Fox, through whose mediumship the manifestations first took place. She was asserted to be a decided humbug. What grounds there are for this assertion can be judged by reading the account now being published in the *Spiritual Times*.

But after all, admitting that Mr. Mompesson (a magistrate) palmed a hoax upon the public—that Mr. Wesley and all the family, including the house-dog, were deceived—that Kate Fox was an impostor—that the people at Romney Marsh smashed their household effects for no conceivable object—that the witnesses who deposed to the appearance of Mrs. Downing and Allen Pierson have combined to palm a lie upon the public, or were themselves deceived, all this would not affect one iota of the phenomena I have myself witnessed, and at times still witness, which cannot be referred to natural causation. This, at any rate, is not the kind of evidence your correspondent alludes to. "What somebody heard, what somebody told somebody else."

There is one more point I wish to refer to, which is this: There is an impression abroad, that, though

sincere in the matter myself, I am "influenced by
others who have not the same honourable intentions."
This certainly is not paying me a very high compliment.   I beg to contradict entirely this false impression, which I believe to have been set afloat as one of
the many phases of opposition.   I wish it to be distinctly understood that the course I pursue is entirely
independent.   I act on my own judgment, my
conviction having been the result of evidence too
decided to resist.   If there is any responsibility involved I have no desire to shirk it.   Neither do I desire
to claim the merit, if merit there be, of aiding to
spread a great and important truth, though for its
sake 1 have incurred the displeasure of friends and
braved the persecution of foes.

But admitting, for argument's sake, that I am mad,
or the dupe of others, is such the case with everybody
who believes in Spiritualism ? is such the case with
the   host   of   men   of   learning,   integrity   and
position, who are its avowed advocates, at the head of
whom stand Louis Napoleon, Professor De Morgan,
Dr. Elliotson, William Howitt, Sir Bulwer Lytton,
and Judge Edmonds of America ? And I would ask, is
it reasonable to suppose that Mr. Home would have
been ordered out of Rome had he possessed no higher
ability than to shove a table about with his foot, or,
as the Uckfield chairman would have us believe, wave
about in the twilight a stuffed glove at 'the end of a
wire ?   The thing is too absurd for belief, and any one
who takes the trouble calmly to reflect a moment
must see it must be so.   Spiritualists may bide their
time ; they   have the argument, and the facts to
support it; and herein lies our strength.   This is
obviously admitted.   What importance would be
attached to anything an humble individual like
myself might say, were it not for the possibility of
the facts on which I take my stand proving true ?
Anything I might advance on my own account, calculated to affect the present order of things, would be
regarded as the idle wind.   But armed with the

argument of facts my words have weight, and the issue will entirely depend upon their establishment. The opponents of Spiritualism, let me assure them, are playing a desperate game. The war they wage is not against me or against any other mortal. The weight of evidence is on our side. They have facts to over-throw; they have truth to overcome, and the angels of God to battle against.

I am, &c.,

Robert Cooper.

Eastbourne, March 11th, 1864.

TO THE EDITOR.

Sir,—Inasmuch as Mr. Cooper has thought fit to drag me, by name, into his letter on Spiritualism in your impression of the 15th instant, will you permit me, in reply, to explain my appearance in that con-nection, and further to repeat my objections to his " facts" in my own words. I may say, *in limine*, that I attended his lecture out of curiosity, and with a wish to hear the conclusions at which a highly res-pectable and intelligent man had arrived from personal investigation of his subject, I took the chair solely in deference to the expressed wish of the meeting, and most certainly with no intention, at the outset of en-tering into any controversy whatever—my sole function, as I understood it, being that of keeping order. As the lecture proceeded, however, I became so painfully conscious that, albeit the audience *might* be listening to the truth, they were by no means getting the whole truth, that I felt it incumbent on me, for the benefit of those present, whose acquaintance with " spiritual " literature was slighter than my own, to offer a few observations upon Mr. Cooper's "facts." I was further moved to do so by the consideration that the town had been placarded with denunciations against all who sought "familiar spirits" and " wizards," and that this wonderful example of the *petitio principii* might possibly have induced some well

meaning but weak-minded people to fancy that these
"manifestations" really had some supernatural element in them.   Having said thus much in explanation
of my presence at Mr. Cooper's lecture, and of the
part which I took, I will pass at once to his letter in
the *Sussex Advertiser* of Tuesday.

And here one thing is most perfectly evident, and
that is that Mr. Cooper utterly ignores the sound old
maxim, *audi alterem partem*, and studiously avoids
reading anything which might shake his new-born
faith.   Mr.   Robert Dale Owen's, *Footfalls on the
Boundaries of Another World* is his gospel.   Everything set down in that edifying work is to be believed,
without cavil, question or examination ; the bare fact
of the appearance of Mr. Owen's name on the title
page, is to silence objection, and stifle enquiry ; and,
in fact, to sum up, this is THE BOOK, and, as they say
on the pill-boxes, " All others are counterfeits." I am
irresistibly led to this conclusion from the remarkable
circumstance that, intimate as Mr. Cooper is with the
detail of the " manifestations " in the Fox family
(the prototypes of the wretched jugglers who "rap" to
parties at so much a head), he has never heard of Mrs.
Norman Culver, or, as he spells it, Cleaver.   Mrs.
Culver's best introduction will be her own deposition,
certified by two witnesses, and made at the town of
Arcadia, in the province of New York.   " I am," she
said, " by marriage, a relation of the Fox girls ; their
brother married my husband's sister.   The girls have
been a great deal at my house, and for about two years
I was a very sincere believer in the rappings ; but
some things which I saw when I was visiting the girls
at Rochester made me suspect that they were deceiving.   I resolved to satisfy myself in some way ;
and sometime afterwards I made a proposition to
Catherine to assist her in producing the manifestations.
I had a cousin visiting me from Michigan, who was
going to consult the spirits, and I told Catherine that
if he intended to go to Detroit it would be a great
thing for them to convince him.   I also told her that

if I could do anything to help her, I would do it cheerfully; that I should probably be able to answer all the questions he would ask, and I would do it if she would show me how to make the raps. She said that as Margaretta was absent, she wanted some one to help her, and that if I would become a medium she would explain it all to me.'' I may say shortly that Mrs. Culver *did* assist in this scandalous fraud, and was taught by Kate Fox her *modus operandi*. "The raps," Mrs. Culver goes on to depose, "are produced with the toes. All the toes are used. After nearly a week's practice with Catherine, showing me how, I could produce them perfectly myself. At first it was very hard work to do it. Catherine told me to warm my feet, or put them in warm water, and it would then be easier work to rap; she said that she sometimes had to warm her feet three or four times in the course of an evening . . . I can rap with all the toes on both feet. . . . Catherine told me how to manage to answer the questions;" and so on, it being quite unnecessary to quote further, as it is tolerably evident why Mr. Owen found it convenient to omit this little *exposé* from his account of the "Hydesville Rappings." The "account in the *Spiritual Times*," does not, somehow, refer to it either; but as this is not yet complete, we must trust to Mr. Cooper to publish Mrs. Culver's affidavit *in extenso* at the conclusion of his account of the Fox family.

With regard to Mr. Mompesson, and the Drummer of Tedworth, Mr. Cooper tells us that Glanvil received an explicit denial that any natural cause had been discovered for the phenomena. Now, I would ask, does Mr. Cooper adopt Glanvil's original account, or Sinclair's versions of Glanvil? and admitting that Glanvil was trustworthy in such a matter (which he clearly was not, being a devout believer in witches *et id genus omne*), what does Mr. Cooper think of that part of the story relating to Mr. Mompesson, having fired a pistol into a heap of wood that was being disturbed, and subsequently finding blood tracks on the

F

hearth and down the stairs? It is proverbially difficult to "get blood out of a stone;" but I should fancy a mere trifle to getting it out of a *spirit!* I do not know to which of John Wesley's "ghosts" reference is made, but if your readers will turn to vol. 7, Boswell s *Life of Johnson*, Croker's edition of 1835, at p. 141, they will find with what contempt Dr. Johnson, one of Mr. Cooper's own authorities, spoke of Mr. Wesley's evidence for his belief in one, in which his brother Charles did not join. My "neglect to observe" certain statements with reference to the Cock Lane Ghost arose from the fact that I derived my information from original sources. If Mr. Cooper will kindly peruse Dr. Johnson's own account in the *Gentleman's Magazine* for 1763, he will find that so far from the "usual noises" being heard when the "girl was "bound and muffled hand and foot," all "scratches and knocks" instantly ceased when "she was required to hold her hands out of bed." Here again Mr. Cooper has been misled by a garbled account of what took place, and, of course, his belief has followed his wish in the matter. I heard, for the first time, at the Uckfield lecture, of the Romney Marsh business; but the details, as given correspond so very accurately with those of a much more famous "event of historic note, known as the Stockwell ghost," that I thought it only fair to the original "spirit" to give the substance of the confession of the servant girl who planned and executed it all. A very full account of the matter may be found in that repertory of information, Hone's *Every-day Book, Year Book and Table Book.* The clothes question I do not care to debate; it struck me as absurd that Mrs. Downing's spectre should have appeared in the ghost of an old cottage straw bonnet; but that was all. Of course it is only consonant with propriety that an apparation should have some attire. A spirit wrapper would seem to be an appropriate one.

With regard to Mr. Cooper's query as to "whether it is reasonable to suppose that Mr. Home would have been ordered from Rome, had he possessed no higher ability than to shove a table about with his foot, or . . . wave about in the twilight a stuffed glove at the end of a wire ?" I may answer, perfectly so. In a city where Januarius' blood liquefies, statues bleed, and pictures wink, does any body conceive that a juggler would be suffered to exhibit for an instant ? Of course not, "Two of a trade never agree." Robin would be ordered off ; Bosco's passport would be returned *instanter* : and even our own time-honoured Jacobs, would never be suffered to make a pudding in a hat. Home is, as rank an impostor, I verily believe, as ever lived ; but the College of Cardinals can't afford even to have a clumsy conjuror's miracles set up in opposition to those of the church. No good Catholic ever dreams of asking for "evidence."

Finally, I come to the array of names of the "avowed" advocates of Spiritualism, with which, however I am by no means paralysed, and, *imprimis*, when did Louis Napoleon "avow" himself an "advocate" of it ? He had, I know, Home at the Tuilleries. as he might have had Robert Houdin ; but when and to whom did he avow that he *believed* in him ? Professor De Morgan has, I think, not yet "avowed" himself by name as an advocate of Spiritualism. I should grieve sincerely to see him add one more to his own "Budget of Paradoxes." Of Dr. Elliotson I would speak only with unaffected respect. I think as highly of his integrity as I do meanly of his judgment. Mr. Howitt has long been known as a discoverer of remarkable specimens of equine nidification. Sir Bulwer Lytton is a man of highly cultivated ,intellect, and a clever novelist, but scarcely one who would be selected to make an experiment. Judge Edmonds may be a very good judge, but, unfortunately, we can only hear of him in England at second or third-hand. So much for Mr. Cooper's list. Now I will myself promise to believe in spiritual manifestations when he can add to it the names of Lord Brougham, Sir John Herschel, Professor Faraday, Mr. Airy, the Astronomer Royal, Professor Tyndall, Professor Huxley, Sir David Brewster, and Sir Charles Lyell.   Here are men whose whole lives have been spent in experiment and investigation, who would come to the consideration of the alleged phenomena with all the advantage of their long scientific training, and who, at all events could not be duped by the professional rappers and darkened rooms, nor—predisposed like Mr. Howitt and Sir Bulwer Lytton to mysticism—accept whatever was told them without enquiry.

Let me in conclusion earnestly recommend all who wish to know what rank humbug spirit-rapping is to read an account of a visit to Mrs. Hayden, a medium, in vol. 6, p. 217 of *Household Words*.   Of another to Mrs. Marshall and her niece, in vol. 3 of *All the Year Round*, p. 375 ; another article at p. 540 of the same Vol.   One in Vol. 7, p. 217 of *Household Words*, and articles in Vol. 11, p. 153, 15, p. 217, and 17, p. 580. If, after the perusal of these, they are willing to receive as " evidence " Mr. Cooper's spiritual narratives, they will only illustrate the truth of what Butler says in Hudibras, that

> " Surely the pleasure is as great
> Of being cheated as to cheat."

I, am, sir,
            Your most obedient servant,
                        WILLIAM NOBLE.

Forest Lodge, Maresfield.
    17th, March, 1864.

Spiritualism at Uckfield.

TO THE EDITOR.

" All newly-discovered truths have, at first, the lot of struggling against old beliefs, but, in the end, they are always victorious.'.—I H. TICHTE.

" I prefer what has been seen by one pair of eyes to all reasoning and guessing."—DR. CHALMERS.

" I have studied the question of Spiritualism wherever I
have gone (in America) and the result is most satisfactory.
There, the great fight is over, and you hear little compara-
tively said of it, but you will find it in all the churches.   It
has given new evidence, new life, and a new leaven to Christ-
tianity t.iere."—ROBERT CHAMBERS,

SIR,—I must again ask you to allow me to trespass on
your space, the importance of the subject forming my
excuse, for in the words of the *Britsh Standard* in its
review of Mr. Powell's work on Spiritualism :—" The
inquiry is by no means the contemptible thing that
many people wish to consider it.   It deals with
alleged facts, which, if true, are astounding ; and if
false, still they are objects of interest and they ought
to be disposed of."
Captain Noble seems to attach great importance to my
not having studied the subject from his point of view.
"Mr. Cooper," he says, "utterly ignores the sound
old maxim, *audi alterem partem*, and studiously avoids
reading anything which might shake his new-born
faith."   This is true, if by it is meant that I did not
rake up all the ridiculous so-called *exposés* that have
been published, and if what I *have* read is a fair sam-
ple of the rest, I have   no reason to regret not
having read more .   The fact is, I became convinced of
the truth of Spiritualism by actual experience before
reading anything on the subject, except the article in
the *Cornhill Magazine,*   After this, I fell in with one
of those *exposés* which appeared to me so truly absurd
that I did not care to read any more of them.   The
one I allude to was in *Once a Week*, which professes to
account for the rising of a table several feet in the air
by its being lifted by the foot of the medium.   The
window-blind was drawn down by Mr. Home with a
lazy-tongs.   His figure floating through the air was
produced by a small magic-lantern, which he had concealed about his person.   And as to Mr. Home's foot
which touched the shoulder of the narrator as he
ascended into the air, he simply stood upon a chair
near him, and laid his foot upon him.   This is the

childish nonsense that is put forth in the explanation of the remarkable Cornhill *Séance;* and now that Mrs. Culver's statement is submitted to my notice, I have still less reason to regret that I did not trouble myself about such publications. Those who have been to Mrs. Marshall's, and heard the raps produced through her mediumship, like smart blows with the knuckle, on the floor, on the table, on the chair, and suddenly transferred to the walls and ceiling of the room, must come to the conclusion that the old lady must have very wonderful toes to produce those sounds, and fail to see how any amount of soaking in warm water could assist the operation. Truly the objectors to Spiritualism are, after all, more credulous than its believers, for they lend themselves to the belief of anything, however improbable or absurd, rather than " give in to spirit." I fear the noble captain himself has made the mistake he charges me with. His investigations have obviously been *very one sided.* He appears to have fallen into the common error of trying to prove Spiritualism to be false, instead of adopting the more rational course—examining it impartially to see whether it be true.

Capt. Noble trusts that I shall publish Mrs. Culver's affidavit *in extenso* in the *Spiritual Times.* Why did he not tell us the sequel which, as he is so conversant with these matters, must have been well known to him. After giving Mrs. Culver's account, why did he not go on and give the full exposure of Mrs. Culver's own false statement ? The whole of Mrs. Culver's account was known by a further inquiry to be a tissue of the most barefaced lies. The Fox girls were submitted to a committee of ladies, believers and unbelievers, and tested all sorts of ways, even to having them stripped naked and laid on cushions, so that their every slightest motion could be seen by all the ladies, and yet the knockings still went on all over the room. These same Misses Fox, years after (one of them now Mrs. Browne), were tested by the professors of Harvard College, Agassiz amongst them, and the knockings went on all over the room, on the walls, ceilings, &c., quite out of all reach of the young women. No single person has yet been able to detect a single trick in either of these ladies, though they have had many thousand *Séances*, and are at this day in the greatest esteem by all who know them, amongst whom are the highest persons in the United States.

As to Faraday, Lyell, &c., they are good investigators of physical matters, but they are the very worst judges of psychical ones, from their educational prejudices. They are disqualified by their preconceived theories, as much as the most uneducated are disqualified for *their* pursuits. Still worse, they have to a man, refused to examine, storing their inveterate hatred of everything spiritual. Faraday and Brewster, indeed made an attempt to examine these things, and their utter incapacity for such research has become the laughing-stock of all Europe, the scientific world included. Faraday's machinery to shew that it was muscular motion, which immediately went up to the ceiling out of the reach of all muscles, has justly become a by-word all the world over. As for poor Sir David Brewster, what does Dr. Maitland, the learned and witty librarian of Salisbury Cathedral, say in his caustic little work, *Superstition and Science?* —" At Mr. Cox's house, Mr. Home, Mr. Cox, Lord Brougham, and myself (Sir David) sat down to a small table, Mr. Home having previously requested us to examine if there was any machinery. When all our hands were on the table, noises were heard, rappings in abundance, and finally, when we rose up, the table actually, *as appeared to me,* rose from the ground. " Here," says Dr. Maitland, " is one of your men, who, we are told are the best judges, and yet he does not know actually whether a table under his nose does or does not, rise from the ground! Is it on men so grossly and avowedly incompetent to judge of plain matter-of-fact, submitted to their senses, that we are to fix our faith on physical science ?"—p. 76. _ Yet

Lord Brougham, Mr. Cox and Mr. Trollope, on the same occasion, said, "The table *did* rise, and no question."

The best observers are men of plain, common sense, the very worst are scientific men, tied up to materialistic theories. They were such men as our Saviour chose to be the judges of the reality of his miracles. Why does captain Noble believe in Christianity, which had only a carpenter for its founder, and a set of ignorant fishermen and tax-gatherers for its witnesses? Had he been then a Roman centurion on the spot, he would have spit his contempt on Christianity, as the learned Greeks and Romans did, and that for centuries. To them Christianity was a humbug, and worse, as Spiritualism is to the superficial and prejudiced of to-day.

Spiritualism does not depend on *names*, but on *facts*, as Christianity did. And yet it has far more learned and scientific names than Capt. Noble's religion had for centuries. In England we have Drs. Elliotson, Ashburner, and Wilkinson, Professor de Morgan, and others who are as scientific and capable of judging as any Lyells or Tyndals, We have in France the Marquis de Mirville, Baron de Guldenstubbe. As to its phenomena—the Counts Gasparin and Szapary, Favre, Mathieu, Cahagnet, Clever de Maldigny, and a long list of others. In Germany, Goethe, as great a physical philosopher as poet; Dr. Kerner, noted for his electrical and magnetic knowledge; Dr. Gassner, author of a noted work on natural science ; Schubert, the author of the *History of the Soul*, equally famous for its physical as for its psychologic learnings ; Dr. Werner and other great natural philosophers ; Baron Reichenbach, the discoverer of the od-force, and the great authority on the subject of ærolites—men all equal to our Tyndals or Lyells. In Belgium, the witty and profound Jobard, late conservator of the Museum of Industry there. In America, Dr. Hare, whose electrical and chemical discoveries, Faraday has availed himself of ; Professors Mapes and Gray, with a fame equal to any of our scientific professors. &c.&c.

Names are not wanting to Spiritualism to settle any question of evidence, But I again repeat it, it is not on names, but on facts, that it takes its stand, and these facts may be found any day at the firesides of millions all the world over. These facts may be pooh-poohed by clever captains, but they won't budge a foot for an army of soldiers ; and whether they believe in them or not, they will continue to exist, and grow, and spread, in calm defiance of the world's contempt or of its favour. If Capt. Noble can only believe on the faith of names, his opinion is just as valuable on this question as that of the mother of Cuddie Hedrigg was on winnowing machines in her day—who would not let Cuddie work in a barn with such an impious machine that set aside God's own winds. Spiritualism will manage to go on without the intellect of mere conventionalism.

It is hardly necessary to allude to Capt. Noble's summary disposal of the names I gave as men of note among spiritualists. There is one name, however, among the list, to which I would refer, before closing this letter—William Howitt, whose literary fame and moral worth are as well recognised in America as in England and Europe, and who perhaps has done more for Spiritualism in this country than any other individual. William Howitt, a mystic ! Truly, there is nothing in his writings to indicate it. On the contrary, in every sentence we discover the honest, bold, common-sense, and uncompromising champion of truth—a fine specimen of the Saxon, who says with regard to Spiritualism, " If they can *put* it out, let them. I, for one, will say, ' Thank you,' if they do, for I have no notion of believing in anything that can be put out." No sir, William Howitt is not the man to be a discoverer of remarkable mare's-nests. Such are much more likely to be found at Maresfield !

I remain

ROBERT COOPER.

Eastbourne, March 26th, 1864.

[We must decline to insert any further correspondence on this subject, as we cannot allow our columns to be made the medium of a controversy on
Spiritualism. Ed. *S A.*]

I have already alluded to the publicity given to
Spiritualism by the press. This last correspondence had perhaps served to ventilate the subject
better than anything that had preceded it, and the
public had the arguments, both for and against,
placed before them ; but I always found the Editors much more ready to admit articles against,
Spiritualism than in its favour, and I generally
found that when I was getting the best of the argument, which I always did, for the simple reason that I had truth on my side, it was intimated
that "the correspondence must now cease." As an
example of this unfairness, in the affair of the
Hailsham Ghost, Mr. Powell and I were both at-
tacked and we both replied. This produced another letter from One Hard of Belief, but a second
letter was refused on the ground that two letters
on our side had already been published. In consequence of this one-sided conduct, I determined
to start a paper of my own, which I did under the
title of the 'Spiritual Times and Weekly News.'
Five numbers only appeared in this form, and the
title was then altered to 'Spiritual Times,' and the
contents restricted to spiritual and kindred topics.
This was printed for several weeks at Eastbourne,
but, the bulk of our subscribers and contributors,
being spread over England and the major part of
them living in London, it was thought advisable
to have the paper printed in London which was
consequently done. But of this more anon.

Our *Séances* were continued, but not in a regular manner, and were for the most part composed of our own family circle : occasionally however they were attended by others who desired evidence of the spiritual facts or who were prompted by motives of curiosity. The communicating intelligences were generally our own spirit friends. The question of indentity is undoubtedly a difficult one even to experienced Spiritualists. I have had, however, the most satisfactory proofs of identity in the case of my wife, and feel as certain of it as if I saw her standing before me in an embodied form. The communications were perfectly characteristic of herself and when made in writing exactly corresponded with her original chirography. Besides, on one occasion, she addressed me by a name she was in the habit of calling me, which name I had not thought of for years, and I did not at first recognise it. This name has frequently been repeated. I am of opinion that it is by no means uncommon for spirits to personate others, either for the purpose of deceiving, or in consequence of the one desiring to communicate not being able, from some cause, to do so. I believe also that, in the case of professional mediums, the communications are often made by the spirits that attend these persons, and that the information given is obtained by reading the mind of the visitor. Doubtless there are exceptions to this, but I consider this to be true in nine instances out of ten. In the case of the Marshalls and the Davenports there are companies of spirits whose work it is to give the manifestations. These spirits are well known to the mediums, even their names. The Davenports claim to have a dozen concerned in their manifestations, but they are only acquainted with two or three of them.

In addition to our own spirit friends we were frequently visited by spirits of whom we had no knowledge whatever. On one occasion we had a spirit who gave his initials *L. S.* On my asking for his name in full, *Laurence Smith* was written. I next asked him to communicate. This for some time he refused to do. At length the words *The letters for communicating* were written. Hereupon, I procured the alphabet and pointed to the letters, when the following sentence was signalled out:—

I once was a dentist and lived at Clapham. I failed in business and went to live in France where I died of the cholera.

I then said "Have you ever communicated in this way before?"

No.

"Would you like me to communicate with any of your friends?"

No, my friends used me very badly, was the reply. This spirit in the course of the day wrote his name again, adding the date of his death which corresponded with the number of years he said, in the morning, he had been in the spirit world. After this he was frequently present and used to indite short sentences such as the following:—

I hope you will have a great many people at your lecture. I wish you success. I take great interest in your affairs.

Our home is a happy one. L. S.

I once had two little babies that died; they are with me.

Another spirit came who declined to give his name, but said he was very unhappy. I asked him to tell me the cause of his unhappiness, but this he would not do, saying *I do not want to*, and on my asking him again, he said *I tell you I do not want to, is not that enough?*

Some spirits however would not hesitate to tell the cause of their trouble, and would indite sentences seeming to imply that we could benefit them by praying for them. Thus one said—

Do all you can for me, and God will bless you.

A spirit who gave the name *Adéle Omersis* came to us one day. In answer to my questions she stated that she used to live in Bloomsbury Square, where she died of consumption, some years ago, and on being asked, whether she was a good or bad spirit, replied *Middling.* On the following day she came again and wrote :

Je ne suis pas fausse, mais je ne dirai rien aujour d'hui.

One Humphrey Short used to visit us, and was in the habit of making communications of a religious character, such as the following :—

From the earth I was taken to live with the spirits in their world. At first I felt afraid to die, but when I saw the saints in glory it was only like throwing off the earthly crust and putting on the spiritual form, so you must not be afraid to die, but prepare to meet your God.

Beware of all earthly snares, and look towards that which is Heavenly.

You must try and do your duty in this world and you will be rewarded in the next; the corruptible will put on incorruption and the mortal will put on immortality in the last day.

The old clergyman's spirit who used so frequently to visit us, wrote the following :—

As the stars shine out from the darkened sky, so it is that the spirits descend to earth to open the veil of mystery. They take the mist from our eyes, and then we behold the glories, beauties and realities of Spiritualism.

Two circumstances I must not omit to mention. There were two clergymen's widows residing in the town, one of whom had recently lost a son, and the other a husband. These two departed spirits were constantly in the habit of manifesting at our *Séances.* I at length asked them whether they would like their friends to be present to witness the manifestations; they replied in the affirmative. I consequently spoke to the ladies on the subject, and they expressed their willingness to attend a *Séance*, remarking that they knew nothing of the matter, and were disinclined to believe anything of the kind. At the *Séance* the table moved in a more vigorous manner than we had before seen it, which drew forth from the lady who had lost her son, such expressions as these, " How wonderful," " How extraordinary." Presently the spirit soon signified his wish for the alphabet, and then rapped out—

When the Lord took me from this state I knew I should be happy.

The table then tipped to the other lady, and this communication was made to her—

May the blessing of God be upon you,

and the recipient burst into tears. It may be well to remark that the lady who had lost a son, holding the ordinary orthodox theologic views, was in doubt about his happiness, in consequence of his being called away suddenly. It would appear that the spirit, knowing the doubt that existed in his mother's mind, was anxious to remove it, and having done so and assured her of his happiness, wafted his flight to higher spheres, for it is remarkable that he never visited us again; neither did the husband of the other lady.

One day after dinner a child whom we knew said, *Diner din, I liked diner once ; little Charlie.*

A spirit wrote on one occasion in a language we did not understand and signed his name ; a very peculiar and characteristic autograph. The next day he came again, and again wrote his name, which exactly corresponded with that of the previous day. He said he was Portuguese. In the autograph of Laurence Smith there was a peculiarity in the formation of the letters which was always the same whenever produced.

A spirit purporting to be George Fox, the celebrated Quaker, paid us a few visits. He signalised himself by writing a characteristic letter to "Friend Howitt."

I might thus go on enumerating similar experiences, but must restrict my observations to a few cases involving some peculiar and noteworthy features. The first I will mention is this. My daughter's mediumship was principally confined to writing; in this she was as good a medium as I have met with in my subsequent investigations, the excellency consisting in the communications that were made through her, being pure and simple, and free from the idiosyncracies of her own mind. Occasionally, however, indications of the drawing faculty would be developed ; but these were, for the most part, scarcely worthy of notice. One circumstance I cannot pass over without recording. We were sitting round a table one evening when the hand of the medium was seen to be engaged in forming a sort of design, which none of us could at first comprehend. When nearly completed, my youngest daughter, who was looking over the shoulder of her sister, exclaimed, "Why it's my collar," and, sure enough, on comparing it with the collar round her neck it was found exactly to correspond, not only in the particular pattern, but in the number of them that composed the collar. Although my daughter was not what is known as a drawing medium, her magnetism appeared to be sufficient to develope the latent faculty in others. Thus, calling one day on a clergyman and his lady, after a little conversation on the subject, a few messages were indited through my daughter's hand. It was then suggested that the lady should try, which she did, but after holding the pencil for some minutes no apparent effect was produced. My daughter then placed her hand on the left hand of the lady, and in a few moments the hand holding the pencil, was seen to be convulsively agitated, and it then began to draw little sketches consisting of landscapes and flowers. The lady said they were done without any volition on her part, in fact she did not know what they were going to be whilst they were in the course of formation.

I have already spoken of being awoke by spirits just as I was falling to sleep. I will now mention another circumstance which occurred to me in the night. The experience of all times proves that the organization of some persons is more susceptible of spiritual influence when asleep than when awake, and in this state they become the subject of visions, dreams, &c.; to quote the words of Job— "In a dream, in a vision of the night, when deep sleep falleth on men, in slumberings on their bed, then God openeth the ears of men and sealeth their instruction." A receptivity to spiritual influence appears to be induced at a certain stage of somnolency; the sound sleep of a person in robust health is not the condition that favours it, but the light sleep of the invalid; hence it is that these results are commonly attributed to a disordered imagination arising from ill health. This state may be promoted by the administration of certain drugs, and the mediumistic power generally may be increased by the employment of them.

Possessing no mediumistic power by which the spirits can manifest through my organization, I nevertheless am susceptible of spiritual impression, and my susceptibility appears to be increased when in a semi-wakeful state. One night—I appeared to be perfectly awake, but I doubt whether I was so; the probability is, I was in some abnormal condition—well, when in this state, awake or asleep, I heard a person in the room. He came to the side of my bed, and leaning over me placed his face against mine. I raised my hands and grasped a head with an old-fashioned cotton night-cap on. I exclaimed in fear "Who is it? a voice replied, *It's your father*, and the apparition, or whatever it was, was gone. The next day, when communicating with the spirits, I asked, in allusion to the occurrence of the previous night, whether it was a dream or whether it was really my father's spirit that had visited me; they said in reply it was his spirit. "What did he come for?" I enquired, *To remind you of him* was the answer. In addition to the seeming reality of this occurrence—for the sounds of the footsteps, the flesh-like feel of the face, the distinctness of the voice, all had the effect of reality, differing entirely from a dream—it is worthy of remark that my father, dying when I was young, is but little remembered by me; my principal recollection of him being derived from sleeping with him, when he wore a cap such as I have described. This was the only occasion he ever manifested his presence to me. My mother, however, did so more frequently, but not very often. I am of opinion that the longer persons are in the spirit-world the less inclination they have to return to earth. There are however instances on record where spirits, from some cause, have hung about their earthly abode for two hundred years or more. We hear a good deal from sceptics about mediums claiming to have the power of "calling up" any spirit at will. I need scarcely say that this arises from an entire misapprehension of the subject on the part of sceptics, or from a pretence, either designed or from ignorance on the part of the mediums, to a power they do not possess. They may "call spirits" as Shakspeare says, but no power on earth can compel them to come. I never made it the practice to ask for any particular spirit; I complied with the conditions necessary for the production of the manifestations, and then allowed the spirits to present themselves as they thought proper, never attempting to exercise any control over them; and this I am satisfied is the best way to manage these matters.

A Russian gentleman was sometimes present at our *Séances*. Though not a professed believer in Spiritualism he had received evidence of a spiritual character that disposed him to accept the communications which came through the table as genuine. He asserted that when at sea he distinctly saw his sister, who was in Russia at the time, and on his arrival there he found she had died at the time he saw the apparition. At our meetings he used to get into communication with Russian spirits and conversed with them in his own language. One of them volunteered some curious information, to the effect that the late Czar committed suicide by taking poison, mentioning the kind of poison and other particulars.

A young lady who was on a visit to Mr. Powell came to my house one evening. She had never witnessed any manifestations, and in fact knew but little of the subject. In the course of the *Séance* she became under spirit influence and gave evidence of strong mediumistic power. She asserted that she could see a spirit whom she recognised. On retiring to bed she could not sleep on account of the furniture in the room being in a state of locomotion. Being alarmed, she called Mrs. Powell to sleep with her, and they then both saw several articles of furniture in motion. The next day she received communications through her own hand and, afterwards, had some very curious and interesting experiences. I believe she did not cultivate her medium powers to any extent, for on her return home, the subject met the disapproval of her friends, but the spirits gave occasional evidence of their presence in spite of their objections.

It has hitherto been the custom to regard all such events as I am considering, by those who admit them at all, as supernatural, but it will be found that the term is hardly a correct one when the facts in question are viewed from a scientific point of view and in the light of modern experience. That higher and more recondite laws than those we are ordinarily familiar with come into operation is undoubtedly true, but that any breach of law is involved in their production there is no ground for supposing. Viewed in this light, one of the most formidable objections of the materialist, who denies the possibility of infraction of any natural law is done away with, and the most thorough sceptic in these matters requires only a reasonable amount of evidence or reliable testimony to induce him to accept the spiritual phenomena.

In order properly to observe spiritual manifestations it is necessary to secure conditions. In addition to having a person through whose organization the spirits can operate, there are other points to be observed, such as the harmony of the circle, the state of the atmosphere, and the amount of light; and above all the spirits must be present and willing to act, for it is a mistake to suppose that they are always present or that they will produce manifestations without a purpose. In the course of what I shall further advance one or two remarkable instances will be given in proof of this and I will now mention a case illustrating the importance of suitable conditions.

One evening we were seated round the harmonium engaged in singing and not thinking at all about spirits, when my daughter said, " The spirits are here, they will not let me sit still." Upon which I said we would finish our piece and then hear what they had to say, On the completion of the music, we turned to the table and it was then intimated that they wanted us to go to Mrs. Tebb (a lady on a visit to the town who possessed mediumistic powers.) I said in reply, " It's late and the weather is stormy and Mrs. Tebb is not expecting us." *Do go*, they said, *we can give you good manifestations to night, the conditions are right.*

I said, "You must excuse us; we really can't

go to night." After repeating the request for us to go, and on my positively declining, they rapped out, *Then we go sorrowing.* It may be well to observe that the weather at this time was stormy, with sudden wind squalls and heavy showers of rain and hail, accompanied by thunder and lightning.

I have already spoken of the advice given to my children producing a salutary effect on them. On the occasion of my daughter's birthday we held a *Séance* at which a few friends were present. The physical demonstrations were unusually powerful, the large dining table being raised a foot in the air and also moving without contact. A request was made that a communication should be given suitable to the occasion; the answer was *Not now, when we are alone—to-morrow at three o' clock.* At the time named we were on the Downs at Beachy Head. We sat down on the grass and immediately received the following beautiful and appropriate message

I am here. I trust you may grow up to be a blessing to your dear Papa, brothers, and sisters, and all the kind friends around you. May you ever love and serve your maker, and when you look around on these beautiful works of nature, you see in them the love God has had for you, poor sinners. O look higher and may you ever, my darling child, look up to Jesus as your father and counsellor. Pray to him dear one. Each year may you ever feel that he is nearer to you and try, dear Mary, to worship him and do not think too much of these earthly things, but look higher, higher, higher.— E. Cooper.

I will only mention two or three more incidents and then pass on. My daughter being ill was visited by the spirits as she lay in bed. They told her what had made her ill, and gave directions to promote her recovery saying to her at the same time words full of kind and affectionate sympathy. They also reproved one of my sons for not controlling his temper, and, on an array of photographs being displayed of different members of the family, they gave an opinion as to which was the best portrait of each individual.

Thus matters went on, till the month of April, not a day passing without receiving communications from our spirit-friends—if we happened to forget them they did not forget us—when they began again to urge me to lecture. This I declined to do on the ground that there was a difficulty in getting audiences without exhibiting manifestations. But the spirits were as importunate as in the first instance, and at every *Séance* made urgent requests for me to give some more lectures; the requests being couched in such words as these, *When are you going to do what your dear wife asks you?* At length I consented, and forthwith arranged to deliver lectures in several towns in a westerly direction commencing at Brighton. Having done this I received this remarkable communication, *I have done my work and shall now only come on special missions.*

"What work do you mean"? I asked.

Establishing this great fact in your mind.

From this time the visits of our spirit friends ceased to be made with any degree of regularity, but were as angels' visits are said to be, "few and far between". The anniversary of my wedding day occurred soon after the above incident when my wife neither forgot me nor the event, but addressed me as follows ;—

I am dead and yet alive. My body is in the ground but my spirit enjoys everlasting happiness in heaven.

I well remember the time when we were marri d, how happy I was ; but I am far happier now, and if you follow the footsteps of Jesus you will enjoy the same everlasting happiness. Farewell dearest; we part but for a time to meet again in a world of bliss.

CHAPTER VIII.

Lecture at Brighton—A clerical opponent—Affray at Southsea—Lectures at Ryde—A scientific witness— Ventnor—Southampton, &c.,

I commenced my lecture tour at Brighton and had an audience of about two hundred persons, most of whom were the upper classes. I was attentively listened to, and the whole passed off without interruption beyond a demand or two being made to "see something;" one gentleman asking me to make a table go up in the air then and there for his satisfaction; upon which another got up and said he had not come with the expectation of seeing any experiments, a lecture only having been announced. This remark of course, had a better effect coming from one of the audience than from myself. My lecture being finished a clerical looking gentleman, who during the lecture I took for a bishop but who turned out to be the Rev. Robert Ainslie the Unitarian minister of the town, mounted the platform and commenced by saying that he had the day before spoken to his congregation about the subject of my lecture, and recommended them to come and hear me for he did not think I was fairly treated at Lewes. I, of course, admired the speaker's candour and sense of justice and began to think I had made an important convert to the views I was propounding. But I soon found I was mistaken, and discovered that his real object in adopting the apparently liberal course towards me was, not that his congregation might be edified by hearing me lecture on Spiritualism, but that they might witness his dexterity in setting me down. He then commenced a long tirade against Spiritualism displaying entire ignorance of the subject and offering the usual materialistic objections. "Shew me a table in motion" said he "and I will very soon shew you what makes it move". He said he once saw something in the moonlight which he took for a ghost but which turned out to be a donkey or something of the kind. This of course, had great weight with the audience and produced much laughter. The Rev. gentleman brought his remarks to a climax by asking in an emphatic manner "Do you think the Divine Being would permit a happy spirit to leave its ethereal home to count a dozen nuts?" As a concluding piece of folly one gentleman proposed to the audience to hold up their hands to ascertain how many converts I had made, and as none held up their hands, he chuckled with delight, forgetting that I commenced my lecture by saying that I did not expect, by my remarks, to make converts—that my aim was to induce investigation.

The next lecture I gave was at Southsea in the large Portland Hall, at which an incident occurred of which the following is an account taken from one of the local papers:—

The following amusing conversation then took place

between Mr. O'Reilly and the lecturer :—Mr. O' Reilly : Can you do anything of this sort now ?—(Laughter, and hear, hear.)—Lecturer : I am not a medium.—Mr. O' Reilly :   But if there is a medium here ?—Lecturer : I don't think the experiments are suitable for a public audience.—(A   laugh.)—Mr. O'Reilly : How do you know ?—Lecturer : I judge from the experience I have had in the matter.   The spirits are not always under control.—(A laugh.)—Mr. O' Reilly : Why not try.—Lecturer : We will try if there is a medium here.   I tried it once at a public meeting, and it was successful.—Mr. O'Reilly : Can anything of the kind be done now ?—Lecturer : Not unless there is a medium present. —Mr. O'Reilly: How do you know a person is a medium ?—Lecturer : That is only done by actual trial. I and several others tried one night, and we were about to give it up in despair, when up went the table.—Mr O'Reilly : I suppose you've heard of the man who made an extraordinary leap in Rome, and when asked if he would repeat it, said he was not in Rome.—(Laughter.) —A gentleman near the platform, who had frequently manifested his approval of the lecturer's remarks, rose and said he could testify to the truth of a great deal of the lecturer's statements.—Mr. O'Reilly said he had come there for information.—The gentleman near the platform : We don't come here to listen to you, we come here to listen to the lecturer.—Mr. O'Reilly : I suppose not, and the less you say the more you'll shine—The gentleman near the platform here rose with great warmth, and was about to rush upon 'Mr. O'Reilly, when he was seized by two ladies; who begged him to compose himself.

The next day I visited Gosport where I found the whole attention of the town taken up by a gentleman, who assumed the name of " Parallax," promulgating a new theory respecting the shape and size of the earth and the distance of the heavenly bodies; in fact he endeavoured to make out that our system of astronomy was wrong altogether. I learned on my arrival that the room I had engaged to lecture in had been nightly filled for several days past by an eager crowd interested in listening to a debate which had been got up by "Parallax," between himself and some naval officers. The result was as I expected. The public had had enough of lectures on either mundane or super-mundane themes and I obtained no audience; they were too much interested about the shape and size of this world to care to hear anything about the future one. Instead of lecturing I adjourned to the house of the Independent Minister, who had come to the Hall to hear me, and had some conversation with him on Spiritualism. The next day the Rev. gentleman witnessed some writing through my daughter, the comunicating intelligence professing to be a former member of his congregation. This gentleman, like most of his cloth, seemed more inclined to question the propriety of Spiritualism than to doubt its facts, and like most persons had a ghost story to tell. He told me that the house he occupied before he came to Gosport had the reputation of being haunted; that sounds like a man walking up and down stairs with loose slippers on were perfectly heard. This was supposed to be the spirit of the late occupant of the house. A very remarkable circumstance occured which could never be accounted for. One day whilst the family were at prayers a loud noise, as if a tray full of china and glass were suddenly let fall, was heard in the adjoining room, and though an immediate search was made to see what was the matter nothing could be found to account for the sound which had caused the alarm.

I next visited Ryde in the Isle of Wight. Here

I found a friend to the cause—the first I had met with in my travels. Mr. Broderick the author of an excellent little book "Is it true?" is he to whom I allude. His little book was then in manuscript and my opinion was asked as to the advisability of publishing it. I pronounced favourably and think still better of it now that I have read it in print. To my surprise Mr. Broderick, although very well acquainted with spiritual matters and on which he had written an excellent book, had never seen any manifestations; accordingly I invited him to my rooms at night intending to hold a *Séance* that he might witness some phenomena if any could be elicited. We sat at a table and succeeded in getting it to move, but nothing very astonishing took place. He was however informed by the spirits that he was a medium, which turned out to be true, and in the appendix of his book he has given a very interesting account of his development.

I delivered my lecture at the Victoria Rooms and was listened to very attentively. At its close a gentleman, who, I was afterwards informed was a doctor, asked, in reference to the levitation of Mr. Home, to which I had referred, whether I believed the law of gravitation was suspended to produce the result. In reply I told him I did not believe anything of the kind; the phenomenon was produced by a force coming into operation which overcame the law of gravitation. Hereupon a gentleman named Paul arose and said he could corroborate my statements so far as the table phenomena were concerned, for he and his brother had paid a visit to Mrs. Marshall and they were both satisfied of the reality of the phenomena, but questioned their spiritual origin. He then went on to describe how he had requested a table to remain suspended in the air while he counted twenty which was done. Mr. Paul illustrated the suspension of the table by holding a chair in the air. He had also written to Professor de Morgan, whom he knew very well, and received the following reply :—

"I am perfectly satisfied that phenomena such as you describe are genuine, and this from what I have seen and heard on evidence which I cannot doubt. What they arise from I cannot tell. The physical phenomena you describe are beyond all explanation ; but still there may be physical forces we know nothing of. The mental phenomena are far more difficult. There must be, so far as we can see, some unseen intelligence mixed up in the matter. Spirit or no spirit there is, at least, a reading of one mind by something out of that mind."

Mr Paul had, previous to my visit to Ryde, read a paper before the Philosophical and Scientific Society of the town on the subject. This is published in Mr. Broderick's book and is well worth perusal.*

Proceeding to Ventnor I gave my lecture there. The clergyman of the parish was present and was an attentive listener. When I had finished he expressed belief in my sincerity, condemned Spiritualism as satanic, and advised his " dear friends " to have nothing to do with it.

I next went down to Cowes and thence to Southampton where I made the acquaintance of " Parallax." This gentleman evinced great interest in Spiritualism, and seemed much more inclined to accept my views concerning the next world than I was his relating to this. The lady with whom I lodged told me of some spiritual

* Is it True ? Pitman.

experiences she had had.   One was to this effect.
She dreamed she attended a funeral.   The *cortége*
passed through a long avenue of trees, and the
burial took place by the side of a cyprus tree.
The locality was unknown to her at the time.
Her dream was realized in every particular.

Another old lady in whose house I lodged at
Havant told me of a curious circumstance that
happened to her husband.   He possessed a boat,
and when he went to it he said he saw himself
sitting in it.   In a few days the boat was run
down by a revenue Cutter and its owner drown-
ed.   Visiting other towns on my return home,
where nothing worthy of note occurred, I completed my lecturing tour, which, though not so
successful as I anticipated, was doubtless the
means of bringing the subject, through the press,
to the minds of thousands ; full and accurate
reports of the lectures appearing in many newspapers.

CHAPTER IX.

A few more circumstances of my earlier experiences remain to be recorded before passing on
to the main object of this book—my experiences
with the Davenport Brothers.

Mr. Conklin, a medium from America, being
on a visit to this country, I availed myself of the
opportunity to give some friends evidence of
spirit action through his mediumship. At my
request he came to Eastbourne, and I invited
about a dozen persons interested in the subject to
witness the manifestations that take place in his
presence. All these persons were, I believe, convinced of the reality of them. Mr. Conklin is
what is known as a test medium. I also invited
two Lewes gentlemen, who were connected with
the press, to have the evidence Mr. Conklin could
give, and the following is an account of their experience as published at the time.

Mr. J. B. Conklin, the American test medium, has given us some very remarkable evidences of his mediumistic powers. He was entertained by Mr. R. Cooper, at whose house some very conclusive illustrations of spirit presence have been given. On Saturday evening a number of gentlemen who had formerly, at a public meeting, been elected to make some investigations along with Mr. Cooper, with a view to test the reality of the alleged phenomena, were favoured with a sitting. Mr. Conklin desired them, one by one, to sit at the opposite end of the table to himself, and to take a number of pieces of paper, write on each the degree of relationship of some friend or relative deceased. This was done. and the paper rolled up into pellets and thrown into the centre of the table. The medium then picked out one of the pieces of paper and threw it towards the person giving the test. A number of other pieces of paper, with the christian names of the departed were inscribed ; the papers being rolled up in the same manner, the medium picked out one as before. Afterwards the diseases—the ages—and the places of death were each written and made into pellets ; and singular enough the medium picked out of each lot a single pellet. When the selected pieces were opened they were generally found to correspond

Mr. Jas. Bates and Mr. Alfred Duplock, of Lewes, two gentlemen who had been promised by Mr. Cooper when he was at Lewes, that he would give them an opportunity of witnessing some illustrations of spirit power, were next favoured with a sitting, at which some extraordinary,and confessedly to them unaccountable, phenomena took place.

Mr. Bates tried the pellets, and having used twelve pieces of paper was wonderfully astonished to find that the medium picked out three of the pellets containing the degree of relationship—christian name, and the age of one dead. He was the more staggered at this from the fact that he had written most of his pellets in shorthand. A similar process was adopted with Mr. Duplock, with nearly the same success

At a third and last sitting a gentleman desired to have the name given of an enveloped photograph after he had failed in getting the right age of his deceased relation, but had obtained the place of death. A number of eight or nine names was written—the table signalled one "Robinson;" and the communicating spirit persisted in having it "Robinson." Mr. Cooper was requested to close his eyes and draw a black-lead pencil slowly along the paper over the written names. He did so; when the pencil reached "Robinson" the table ambled. The paper containing the names was then turned over, the blank side uppermost. Mr. Cooper closed his eyes again, drawing his pencil over the paper as before —the table knocked—Mr. Cooper stopped, and to the astonishment of most of the company his pencil was on the name "Robinson" again. Mr. Bates then took the paper containing the names—tore the names separately off, and made them into pellets. It was impossible that any one could say which pellet contained the written name Robinson; but singularly enough the table knocked out assent when the right pellet was held up. The name Robinson was signalled altogether seven times in different ways. During this sitting five of the company had unmistakable touches— taps or grips from invisible hands. We ourselves were four or five times taken hold below the knee.

Mr. Duplock felt a pressure on his knee, and put his hand down to feel the cause, when he had the satisfaction of feeling a spirit hand take hold of his. Miss. Cooper and a Miss Peel each had several grips, or pulls and Mr. Conklin was dragged from his chair partly under the table.

During these sittings two tables—one weighing about 80 lbs., and the other about 112 lbs.—were several times raised by spirit-power above *terra firma.*

Mr. Conklin's visit to Eastbourne is very satisfactory. He appears an unassuming, earnest, intelligent man, and from the marvellous medium powers he possesses, must be regarded as a man among men."

Soon after this Mr. Conklin went to Glasgow, where he experienced very rough and unfair treatment. A pamphlet, written by a Mr. Paterson, professed to be an exposure of the whole affair, but according to the writer's own statements there are many things, connected with the answering of questions, difficult to account for. The lifting of the table was explained by suggesting that the medium had hooks concealed in his sleeves!

Some time after the events I have recorded took place we had some very singular experiences, a brief account of which, I will endeavour to give. Strange and unaccountable noises were heard in my house at times during the day— sometimes rappings; at other times sounds like sweeping with a brush; and once sounds like a small silver bell were occasionally heard in the adjoining room, and on going there to see what occasioned them, they were heard in the room that had been vacated. At night the noises increased to such an extent that it was difficult to sleep. I was awakened by them and my children were kept awake and had a light burning nearly the whole of the night. They continued at intervals throughout the following day, and were renewed with increased vigour at night. For about two hours there was the sound as of a person walking up and down the stairs moaning. The servants on going to their bedroom heard the name *Sarah*, which was the name of one of them, distinctly whispered. The noises continued at intervals again the next day, and increased to such an extent in the evening that the servants said they were afraid to be in the kitchen. It then occurred to me that the spirits desired to make a communication, and accordingly I took my daughter to the kitchen, and we sat at the table and very soon ascertained what was the matter. A spirit who purported to be the mother of one of them wanted her to come to the table and receive a communication. This she refused to do; she had been advised to have nothing to do with it, she said she "did not believe it was spirits." After some persuasion she was at length induced to sit at the table, when communications were written out by her own hand. The purport of these communications was to warn her against some young man with whom she had become acquainted. After this the servants went to their bedrooms when the noises were as bad as ever, and in addition they felt hands pressing all round the bed. In the morning this curious ⌊message was given through the girl :—

There shall be great noises in the night, if any man says we are not spirits, he shall be plagued.

The young man was given up, the mother's solicitude was at an end, and from that time the disturbances ceased.

At day break one morning Mr. and Mrs. Hicks were awoke by hearing a sound as if the table were struck with a whip. On looking in the direction of the sound they saw the lower drawer of a chest come a little way out and presently a little farther. Mr. Hicks got out of bed and shut the drawer and on opening it again it made the same noise that had awoke them. This was occasioned by the drawer hanging at first starting. At night I went to Mr. Hick's house and he told me of the circumstance and shewed me the drawer. After trying in vain to find a solution we adjourned to the room below and held a *Séance*, and in the course of the evening the mysterious affair of the drawer was alluded to. I said, "Perhaps the spirits can tell us something about it."

I did it, was instantly rapped out.

"What did you do it for?" I asked.

To set you thinking, was the reply.

Mr. Hicks be it observed was one who, like Sir David Brewster would not "give in to spirit," and referred all the wondrous doings he had witnessed to magnetism and attempted to explain the opening of the drawer by the expansion of the air by heat. Truly there is no credulity like incredulity!

It is a remarkable fact in connection with the manifestations of spirits that at times they cannot even move a table unless it is in contact with the medium, whilst at other times they can operate when no person is near it; thus I have occasionally heard the furniture, in the room where we had been holding a *Séance*, in motion after retiring to bed; and on one occasion we were surprised at finding, on coming down stairs in the morning the front door and the outer door, also the door of the basement floor all wide open. These were all fastened as usual on retiring at night.

One circumstance only remains to be mentioned in connection with my preliminary experiences. A distinguished preacher in London expressed a desire to witness some manifestations. Mr. Powell and I accompanied him to Mrs. Marshall's. After making an examination of the table to be used, we took our seats, with Mrs. Marshall, round the table. Our friend asked for his name to be spelt out, which was immediately done by raps. Neither of the Christian names were known to us, and one is a very peculiar one. Questions were then asked, and answered, more or less to he satisfaction of the inquirer. A guitar was then held in the position of a bass-viol when played on, and the strings were then forcibly thrummed. Two or three specimens of direct writing without visible hands were produced; and on a ring and a tumbler being placed on the floor a clink was heard and the ring was found inside the glass. All these things took place in broad day-light and under circumstances that admitted of no possible trick or deception.

I have thus endeavoured to narrate, in as plain and simple a manner as I am capable of, the principal events of my first few months' experience in Spiritualism. I entered upon its investigation a disbeliever in the supernatural, but (belief being an involuntary action or condition of the mind) the force of facts was so great that a revolution was wrought in my opinions, and the evidence I received resulted in making me a decided and practical convert.

CHAPTER X.

The age of Invention.— Greater marvels. — The Daven-
port Manifestations.— Sicientfic Incredulity.— achie-
ved impossibilities.—High Inspirations.

" This is the patent age of new inventions ".   So
said Lord Byron some forty years ago; and looking
back to that period—the ti me of my childhood—
what many and wonderful inventions have since been
made and brought into use ; Invention has succeeded
invention and discovery discovery with extraordinary
rapidity, and society in every department, has been
more or less affected by them.   At the period referred to the steam engine was invented but not
developed.   Railways were in their infancy and
steamboats a novelty ; the Electric Telegraph was
not dreamt of.   In fact all these mighty agencies
of progress by which work is done, labour saved, and
time and space almost annihilated, may be said to
have had their birth and growth during the last
half century.   The period has also been prolific in
other important matters ; great advance has been
made in the arts and sciences ; inventive genius has
been active in a variety of ways.   Machinery has

been made to supersede manual labour in almost everything. The Sewing machine has superseded the needle: lucifer matches have taken the place of the old-fashioned tinder-box, and are now manufactured to the extent of 500 millions annually. Chloroform has rendered surgical operations painless. The sun paints our likeness with marvellous fidelity, and a portrait can now be obtained for a trifle, more striking and characteristic, than any amount of money could before have purchased. Great Exhibitions were things nnknown to our ancestors and underground Railways above their comprehension. The improved character of our war implements has, owing to their efficiency been the means of settling a dispute in as many days as it would formerly have taken years. Our war ships are made on a principle that would be an enigma to Nelson. The Great Eastern is a grand triumph of naval architecture, exceeding Noah's Ark in its gigantic proportions. The Printing Press sends forth an abundant supply of useful and excellent literature at an almost nominal cost, and the daily Penny Paper is the cheapest thing a penny ever purchased. The Penny Post circulates our letters with despatch and subserves the interests of business and affection, at the same time promoting the cultivation of the intellectual faculties among the masses. Gas has taken the place of candles and oil lamps, and the wonderful discovery of Petroleum renders it probable that Coal gas will be superseded by it; and, in enumerating the most remarkable discoveries of the last half century we must not omit the finding of Gold in California and America, the satisfactory solution of the North West Passage, the unsolved problem of three centuries, the disovery of the sources of the Nile,

and the canal connection between the Red Sea
and the Mediterranean across the Isthmus of Suez.
The extinction of Slavery in America and Serfdom
in Russia are also notable and most important events.
In contemplating all these marvels of the past few
years which are fast ceasing, by their familiarity,
to be regarded as such, and which the ignorant
take as signs of the end of the world, the mind
naturally asks, What next? for we cannot suppose
that we have arrived at the culminating point of
discovery. The probability is, we are on the eve of
something still greater; for like a descending stone
whose impetus increases in its flight, invention, like
jealousy, "grows by what it feeds on;" and therefore, reasoning by analogy, the discoveries of the
past will give impetus to further progressive developments, and, in the future, their effects will be
seen in the physical and moral elevation of the
human race and the amelioration of the condition of
its individual members.

Truly the past half-century has been productive
of many wonders, a hundred times more so than
any similar period of the world's history, and, as if to
crown them, the greatest wonder of all—the direct
action of spirit on matter—is now made manifest
amongst us; for in the spiritual manifestations
vouchsafed to the present age we behold a marvel
unsurpassed in the history of mankind, " the marvel of inanimate matter moving without mortal contact and displaying intelligence, and that intelligence embracing a knowledge of the alphabet, of
reading, writing and arithmetic; speaking in many
tongues and reading human thought, and reveal-
ing to us what purports to be the spirit life with
details which no imagination can fabricate."

In addition to these varied forms of manifestation

adopted by the Spirit World to gain recognition, still more remarkable phenomena are witnessed in the presence of the Davenports; such as playing of musical instruments, the tying and the untying of ropes, the formation of hands and arms, not spectral, but real, tangible and palpable hands, formed in a moment of time and as quickly dissipated into "thin air;" and the extraordinary fact of matter passing through matter. The intelligent mind has only to be satisfied of the truth of these occurrences to be forced to acknowledge that they far transcend in marvellousness all the marvels I have attempted to summarise. These spiritual phenomena are too wonderful to come within the scope of the comprehension of most persons, educated as they have been in the principles of materialistic philosophy; and the result is they deem them unworthy of investigation, set them down as a "popular delusion" of the age, and will not trouble themselves to ascertain whether they are false or true. They form an *a priori* judgment based on their preconceived notions, and ignore the subject as preposterous and absurd; and yet these facts have been demonstrated to the satisfaction of thousands, and it would be a very easy matter to make a long list of names of men, eminent in their respective departments, who, after a lengthened experience and a most critical examination, have acknowledged the verity of the facts and their spiritual origin. That they are rejected by the *quasi* learned is no argument against them; on the contrary, if the past is any criterion to go by in reference to the reception of new truths, the conduct of our so called leaders of the intellectual world in this matter, is strong evidence in their favour, for, as

Mr. Howitt justly observes, "the scientific, the journalists and the clergy have always been the foremost in opposing the nascent truth of the time;" and these are the very men who are the principal opponents of Spiritualism. No new truth is ever ushered full-blown into existence, but, like a flower, has to go through regular stages of development before obtaining general recognition; and as the tender plant is almost beaten down by the force of the contending elements but in the end is invigorated by them, so Truth, though kept down for a season by various forms of opposition, ultimately triumphs and takes deeper and firmer root from the ordeal it has passed. It is the inevitable fate of all new truths to meet with opposition, which generally proceeds, not so much from the ignorant as the learned, who never appear to be made wise by the folly of their predecessors.

One important lesson we learn from the cursory retrospect of past achievements, and that is, that many things that were once deemed impossible are now accepted and familiar facts, having a practical realization in the present. Who, for instance, twenty years ago, would have deemed it possible for a message to be sent from London to New York and an answer received in the short space of an hour or two? and yet it is done; or who a few years ago, would have thought it possible to go from London to Paris in about ten hours? and yet these journies are daily accomplished; or, to take another example, who would have contemplated the probability of a portrait being taken with, in some cases, an almost objectionable accuracy, in the space of a few seconds? yet such is the case. These examples suffice to shew the unwisdom of limiting the possible by

our own standard of experience and knowledge.
He is the wisest man, who, recognising the
complex nature of man and his mysterious
surroundings, refuses to assign any limit as to
what can or cannot be, but like the great Sir
Isaac Newton confesses that he is ''like a child
picking up pebbles on the shore, whilst the great
ocean of Truth lies before him unexplored!'' It
has been well said that ''we are never farther
from the Truth than when we imagine that the
largest amount of human knowledge is anything
but as the light of a taper in the sunshine of the
Infinite, or when we cease to perceive that we are
girt about on all sides by mystery!''

The spiritual phenomena which are now regarded with so much distrust have under the name of
the supernatural, been known in all ages and
among all nations, which may be proved by a
reference to a number of reliable authors. Those
who have not time to make the necessary research-
es for themselves cannot do better than read
Mr. Howitt's '' History of the Supernatural,'' in
which they will find a vast and compendious
collection of well authenticated spiritual facts from
a variety of sources. It will be seen by a reference
to this work that spiritual facts are not confined
to Bible history but, as I have already observed,
are to be found in the history of all nations; and
instead of ceasing, as some assert, at the time of
Christ, have continued in some form or other ever
since. What are known as modern spirit
manifestations, differ from the Spiritualism of the
past in this respect, that they are capable of
being elicited almost at will in the presence of
certain persons; and so true is this in the case of
the Davenports that they rarely fail to get the

manifestations when they desire them, although they are sometimes much more powerful than at others.

I have already stated the difficulty I experienced at my lectures on account of my inability to illustrate them by experiments. Wherever I went there was a demand for manifestations. The public seemed to be under the impression (that is, those were disposed to believe in my statements) that I could " call spirits from the vasty deep " at will and that the manifestations were under control; that the spiritual phenomena in fact could be exhibited with as much facility as dissolving views; but, at that time my experience taught me that there was so much uncertainty about them that it would be unwise to announce anything in the way of manifestations. I had seen accounts from time to time in the American papers of the public manifestations of the Brothers Davenport and I determined to invite them to this country, believing they would supply the want I stood so much in need of. I accordingly wrote to them, and by a curious coincidence I received intelligence of their intended visit to England about the same time my letter must have reached America. About the time of their arrival in this country (Sept. 1864) I was on a visit with my daughter to a gentleman in London who was much interested in the subject of Spiritualism. During this visit two curious circumstances occurred, which, though they have no connection with the Davenports are worth recording. Our host was in the habit of driving us out in his carriage, and one day on passing the Monument, he proposed that we should make its ascent. We did so, and when on the top he suggested that we should endeavour to

get a communication from the spirit world, remarking that it might probably be of an elevated
character. The trial was accordingly made and
immediately the words *Hook it*, were written,
followed by the name *Thomas Hood*. After a brief
interval the following words were written in a
differenthand, *Be charitable ; give a penny to that poor
man.* It was at first thought that the man alluded
to was the man in charge of the monument, but
on enquiring the medium's hand was directed to
the street below, and on looking down we
observed a wooden-legged man soliciting alms—
a fair object of charity. I need not say that on
descending, the wishes of our spirit friend were
complied with. The next day we ascended St.
Paul's, where the following communication was
given :—

*Ye frail children of men, ye worthless generation,
ye whom Jesus died to save, ye are but mites compared
with the Great, Good, and Infinite Being who made
you all. Oh ! bless and praise Him. Oh ! ye
children of men, give Him thanks for all this bountiful
goodness. May the grace of the Lord be with you
Amen.—A Clergyman.*

On being asked his name *Charles Gray* was
given.

CHAPTER XI

The Davenports in London—Herr Tolmaque—First
Séance—Medical critics.

I took an early opportunity, in company with
Mr. K. of calling upon the Davenport party to
make their acquaintance. Just at this time the
first notices of the manifestations appeared in the
newspapers, occasioning great excitement in the
public mind and setting the conjurors on the alert.
The day on which I visited the Davenports, a letter from Herr Tolmaque appeared in the papers
undertaking to do, by natural means, all the Davenports did and more too, if I remember right. It
was written in such a plausible and decided manner that even those favourable to the Davenports
were staggered by it; and Mr. K. with great simplicity took Dr. Ferguson aside and said, "There
is a man who pledges himself to do all the
Davenports do. Now I don't wish to be mixed up
with this matter if it is mere conjuring; tell me
therefore candidly whether it is true or no." I
shall never forget the Doctor's reply. In a solemn
and emphatic manner he said, "IT'S AS TRUE AS GOD."

With this assurance we started off to find Herr Tolmaque to inquire into his pretensions. His address was a coffee house near the Strand, but he was not at home. We afterwards learnt that it was an indispensable condition with Herr Tolmaque to be paid £20 before he would consent to reveal any of his knowledge. This information saved us the trouble of further search after him.

The first *Séance* I attended was at the Hanover Square Rooms, in an upper chamber, about twenty persons being present. On this occasion Dr. Radcliffe and another medical gentleman acted as committee. The manifestations were witnessed by me in silence amidst the sceptical remarks of most of those present. The evidence to my mind was conclusive and I imagined the world would soon become convinced of the reality of the spiritual phenomena. All present were more or less puzzled, and several explanations were attempted. That which found most favour was, that there was a communication with the back of the cabinet, which stood about six inches from the wall. The committee, at the close, looked crest-fallen, for they had evidently come there thinking, as hundreds have done before and since, to unravel the mystery, but had failed to do so. Only the cabinet *Séance* took place, but Dr. Ferguson described the principal features of the dark *Seance*, which were received with much apparent incredulity, especially his allusion to the taking off of Mr. Fay's coat while his hands were fast tied. An account of this *Séance* was published in the *Lancet*, in which the writer made the sapient remark, that there would be no difficulty in accounting for the manifestations if they could understand how the

Davenports could untie and re-tie themselves so quickly! After all, this shrewd criticism is perhaps equal to any that subsequently appeared, if we except that of a writer in the *Field* who suggested that the real use of the boxes in which the cabinet is packed, is to secrete a small boy in, who produces all the wonders.

On leaving the room and reaching the foot ef the stair-case I encountered a number of medical students emerging from the room below, where the Annual Address of one of the medical schools had just been delivered. " What's going on up stairs?" asks one gentleman of another. " Its the Davenports," was the reply. " What's that ?" "Oh, awful humbug; perfect rot ;" and judging from the address recently delivered by Mr. Richard Barwell, F. R. C. S. at the opening of the medical school at Charing Cross Hospital, this is the estimate still formed of the Davenports by the medical profession. Here is what this modern Solon says, " Mesmerism, clairvoyance, electro-biology succeeded each other, and as each experimenter outbids his fellows in the marvellous so the public was stimulated even to the swallowing of Spiritualism and table-rapping. A mind greedy of the marvellous would scarcely be checked by anything, but the limits of absurdity had probably been reached with the idea that disembodied spirits should delight themselves in the company of two mountebanks, hid up in a cupboard playing "Sally come up," or other graceless melodies on a vile guitar or wheezy accordion." This, the professor no doubt thought very clever, and his audience evidently thought so too, for it elicited " loud laughter."

It has been said that a goose that quacks in the

Lancet finding that his blunderbuss misses fire, takes the usual alternative of trying to knock down truth and fracture enquiry with the butt-end. This Professor Faraday at first did in reference to Spiritualism, but latterly he has adopted a different course,—he now prefers giving it a wide berth. Some three or four years ago an arrangement was made for him to witness Mr. Home's manifestations when he required to be furnished with a programme, and as this could not be done he declined to attend. Professor Faraday was invited to the test *Séance* of the Davenports, that took place at Mr. Boucicault's, at which several distinguished persons were present. Instead of asking for a programme in this instance which he might have had, he sent the following letter:—

Royal Istitution of Great Britain.

Gentlemen,—I am obliged by your courteous invitation, but really have been so disappointed by the manifestations to which my notice has at different times been called, that I am not encouraged to give any more attention to them ; and therefore leave those to which you refer in the hands of the professors of legerdemain. If spirit communications, not utterly worthless, should happen to start into activity, I will trust the spirits to find out for themselves how they can move my attention. I am tired of them. With thanks, I am very truly yours,

M. Faraday.

The Brothers Davenport.

The assumption and self-importance displayed in this letter are hardly worthy a great philosopher; but Truth will assert its claims in spite of the Faradays and Brewsters of the time, although spirit be the "last thing they will give in to."

In all ages it has owed more to credulity than to
conceited scepticism and self-sufficient prejudice,
and unfolds before those who watch and wait in
humility sitting like children at the feet of a re-
vered teacher

It will be unnecessary for me to follow the
Davenports in their short, and for the time, successful career in England; my object being to
record the principal incidents that occurred
during my more immediate connection with them.
It will be sufficient then to state that they gave
public *Séances* at the Hanover Square Rooms, and
private ones, almost nightly, at the residences of
the nobility and gentry, to the end of 1864. I,
then, arranged with them to visit Brighton and
several other towns where I had delivered lectures,
and from this time they continued in the provinces
till the *fracas* at Liverpool and Huddersfield occurred.   These organized conspiracies to put the
exhibition down were in a measure successful,
giving, as they did, the impression that the "bub-
ble was burst," and from that time the popularity
of the Davenports began to wane.   They, however exh.bi'e i immediately afterwards with complete
success in London, Cheltenham, and Bath, and
then resolved to visit Paris.

For some time after their arrival in France they
were unable to exhibit in public.   This arose from
inability to obtain the necessary *permit* which was
probably witheld on account of the disturbances
that had occurred in England.   During the time
they were "laying on their oars" *Séances* were
given in private before many distinguished men
and members of the press which caused notices to
appear in the newspapers and some of these were
of a highly sensational character.   A controversy

ensued which was kept up for several weeks and
raised the excitement and curiosity of the public
to the highest pitch; and when at length a public
Séance was announced the Salle Herz was filled
with an eager an excited crowd.   The manifestations had just commenced with every promise of a
triumph, when an emissary of Robin, the
conjuror, stepped on the platform, and, under
pretence of examining the cabinet, tore the rail
that supported one of the seats from its place,
and holding it up before the excited crowd, asserted that he had discovered a secret spring.   Great
confusion ensued which prevented an explanation
being given, and although the Davenports
offered to proceed with the exhibition, the police,
to avoid a row, ordered the room to be cleared.
This affair was of course trumpeted forth as
another exposure, and for the time they did not
know how to make enough of it, but in a few
days they were constrained to admit that "the
exposure of the Davenports had not been so
complete as was at first supposed."   The *Séances*
were continued, but by order of the *Prefect* the
audiences were restricted to sixty persons.   Just
as they were on the point of leaving Paris they
received a summons to appear at the palace of St.
Cloud, where the Emperor and Empress and
a party of about forty witnessed the manifestations with astonishment and at the close expressed
their entire satisfaction.

A few days after, Robin gave his exhibition—a
professed exposure of the Davenports—at the
palace.   It was supposed at the time, by those
who knew the Emperor to be a believer in spiritual phenomena, that his object in sending for
Robin was from motives of policy, but it subse-

quently transpired that it was done to allay the excitement of the youthful Prince, who witnessed the Davenport exhibition and had since done nothing but talk about the "spirits." The Emperor pronounced Robin's performance the greatest rubbish he had ever seen.

While in Paris the Davenports were visited by Hamilton, the successor of the far-famed Robert Houdin, who seems to possess more honesty and candour than the generality of the conjuring fraternity. In a letter addressed to one of the Paris newspapers he says—

"The phenomena surpassed my expectations, and the experiments are full of interest for me. I consider it my duty to add they are inexplicable."

A manufacturer of conjuring apparatus named Rhys, also published a letter in which, after enumerating the conditions under which the Davenport exhibitions take place, says—

" Under the conditions you observe no one has yet produced anything similar to the phenomena 1 witnessed, indeed, I believe it would be impossible."

CHAPTER XII

The Davenports in Ireland.

The visit of the Davenports to Paris can hardly be considered a successful one, taking into account the time they spent there and the few *Séances* that were given. This, following upon the disastrous break-up in England, had a discouraging effect on them and they were almost resolved to return to their own country. At this juncture, knowing the value of their mediumship on account of its capability for public display, I proposed to them to give some more *Séances* in England. To this they assented, and accordingly I arranged with them to exhibit at the Hanover Square Rooms, undertaking the part myself recently enacted by Dr. Ferguson. The *Séances* passed off quietly and successfully, but the attendance was not so good as desired. At this time I was visited by Mr. Lauder from Dublin, who strongly advised me to take the Davenports to that City, assuring me of success. I submitted the proposal to the Brothers, and it was agreed to take the advice of "John," for, be it observed the Davenports never take any important step without consulting their spirit friends. Ira Davenport and I took an early opportunity therefore of adjoining to a dark chamber that we might take the opinion of "John" on the proposed visit to Ireland. We had not been secluded a minute before I was touched on the shoulder, and, in reply to my question, a gruff voice almost too thick to be intelligible, said *Go immediately*; but nothing more could be elicited. It was however afterwards rapped out as we were sitting at the table, *Beware of the shillelaghs*.

It may be well here to observe that the spirits in communicating with the Davenports usually speak in an audible voice. This, I am aware, will be discredited by most persons, but it is nevertheless a fact which numbers of persons, both in America and England, have realized and are as well satisfied of as myself. It will probably be objected that, inasmuch as articulation is produced by the action of the vocal organs on the air,—that in fact it is a mechanical act—it is impossible for a being of a spiritual order to act on the air in such a way as to produce the phenomenon of speech. This is doubtless a valid objection, which I would meet in this way. Spirits exist in a spiritual form, and their power over matter is such as to enable them under favourable conditions, to materialize their forms, or parts of them, the production of hands and arms being of very common occurrence. These hands are, for the time, real, palpable, material hands, and possess the qualities and properties of living, human hands. I have seen the veins and felt the nails on them. They are formed momentarily and are dissipated as quickly. How this is effected we cannot understand ; neither can we how the earth is suspended in space, how the grass grows, how the egg is converted into a chick, or how the food is assimilated and converted into blood. Yet these are all familiar facts, and if the production of spirit forms was as common, it would excite no more wonder than they do. The spirits themselves say it is done by an effort of will. To produce the speaking, the vocal organs are doubtless materialized in the same way as the hands, and if the one be possible why not the other ? As I shall frequently have occasion to allude to conversations held with the spirits during my connection with the Davenports, it will be well, I think, to state a few more particulars with regard to this wonderful fact, so that, if possible, my readers may be satisfied that it is no myth, but a truth that can be established as well as any of the other facts of Spiritualism.

I will first describe the circumstances under which I first heard spirits speak. One evening, just after the Liverpool riot, I was in company with the Davenports, and they said to me, " We are going to have a talk with " John " to-night; he has expressed a wish to speak with us. Will you come and hear what he has to say ?" I readily assented, and, accompanied by Mr. Powell proceeded with them to the Great Western Hotel. The window of a bedroom being darkened for the occasion, we took our seats, the party consisting of the Brothers, Mr. Fay, Dr. Ferguson, myself, Mr. Powell, and a gentleman, a friend of the Davenports, who was residing in the Hotel. The Brothers sat on the bed, Dr. F. in front of them, Mr. Fay by his side and the rest of us sat facing them. The room was a long one, and on a table

at one end was placed the horn used in the
cabinet. The candle was blown out and we sat
about a minute in silence; raps were then heard
on the wall. "Will John speak to us now?"
asked Dr. Ferguson; on which a report took
place as if the table were struck with a heavy
hammer, and the horn on the table was heard to
be in motion. The next minute a shrill female
voice was heard immediately in front of us. It
was like that of a person of the lower walks of life
and talked away, like many persons do, for the
mere sake of talking. It was intimated that it was
"Kate" who was speaking. There was a great
attempt on her part at being witty, but according
to my ideas of such matters, most of what was
said would come under the category of small—
very small—wit. The gentleman present, to
whom I have alluded, was the especial object of
her facetiousness. He, it appears, was in Liverpool at the time the cabinet was smashed, and,
being recognized in the crowd, a fragment of
the broken cabinet was thrust in his face with the
cry, "That's one of them, he ought to be made to
eat it." This episode formed the subject of Kate's
jokes, and she rung the changes on it to a most
ridiculous extent. The horn at length fell on the
floor, and was again raised in the air and a gruff
voice was heard speaking through it. This we
were informed was the redoubtable "John," who,
judging from his salutation had not recovered
from his displeasure at the Liverpool row. In an
earnest and emphatic manner he proceeded to
tell the Davenports how to act in the emergency.
He told them not to take any steps in reference to
the Liverpool affair, but to go on as if nothing
had happened—to go on in spite of every kind of

opposition He told them to put no more
bills out challenging the conjurors—these,
he said, had served a good purpose, but were no
use now, and then, in an authoritative manner
added, *Tell Palmer I want to speak to him. Palmer is
like a bull in front of a steam engine, not so much
courage,* and after a pause, *nor as much sense.*

"Shall we have any more rows, John?" asked
one of the Davenports. *It's very probable.* The
voice then ceased, and the female began speaking
again, reverting to "eating the cabinet." Sounding immediately in front of me the voice asked
Who's this man with the glass eyes?

"That's Mr. Cooper.
And who's this?
That's Mr. Powell." The horn then rested on
my knee and I said "am I to take the horn?"

To which I received the following very ungra-
cious reply, *If you do, I'll knock it about your head.*
We were then wished *Good night* by the invisibles.
A light was struck and every thing was found in
the same position as when the light was extinguished, except the horn which was lying at
our feet.

The readiest explanation of what I have described will be, that I was imposed upon, and that
the alleged spirit voices were the result of ventriloquism; but of this I am the best judge and
am certain such was not the case; besides, my experience has since been much extended in this direction, and if I had any doubt of the genuineness
of this phase of the phenomena at the time, I am
now in a position to speak most positively as to its
reality. These proofs I shall give as I proceed.

Besides, the phenomenon of spirits talking in an
audible voice is not peculiar to the Davenports.

of such an instrument. In his absence the window was darkened, and the fire in the grate extinguished. He procured with the only table of the kind he could find, a ——— in wood. This was placed upon a small table. The two brothers, Ira and William, sat on each side. Mr. X remained upon a chair and Mr. Ferguson and I sat ——— the brothers came in two dresses. The door had been locked, and the light was extinguished.

Observe that here was no question of money, and no interest to deceive. The brothers, for their own sake, wished to ask about the rites, and to be advised respecting the course to be taken in an emergency. Dr. Ferguson had the same interest, while Mr. X and myself were the only other persons present, and either of us had any interest but curiosity. I would observe, also, that I was thoroughly acquainted with the peculiarities of the voices of every person present. As a physiologist, and as an ——— and ———, I have studied the voice and its ———. I also understand ventriloquism, and can produce all its illusions.

The light had not been extinguished twenty seconds when the ——— funnel was heard to ——— on the table, and a voice, at first coarse and indistinct, came from it. Mr. Ferguson said that he was touched several times both with the funnel and what appeared to be the hand of some person, and two large soft finger ends, as they seemed to me, were pressed deliberately upon the back of my hand.

Then commenced a conversation between the voice and Mr. Ferguson, and sometimes Ira. The voice was formed in the funnel, for its metallic ring could be distinguished, but it seemed to be formed not at the small end, but where it begins to broaden. The words were well formed and clearly articulated, but as if by organs somewhat thick and soft, a little like those of a fat person, or a negro. Statements were made, questions answered, and advice given. I do not care to report the words. The persons interested, Mr.

Ferguson and the two Davenports, were told that
they would probably meet with more difficulties, but
that they would be protected as they had been.
The voice was not that of any of the persons in
the room. It was not the ventriloquial voice. Every
voice has its own character. Every observing person
can distinguish an educated from an ignorant man, by
the tones of the voice and modes of enunciation.
Many shades of character are revealed by the speech.
Many think the ear judges better than the eye. . The
blind are thought by some to be as well able to judge
of character as those who see. For my own part I can
never form a satisfactory idea of a person until I have
heard him.

This voice, then, was that of no person I had ever
seen. It was that of a plain, sensible, common man,
rather below the middle class in culture, but earnest,
and, if one could so pronounce from a voice, honest.
If, the room being dark and the door unlocked, a
stranger had entered and spoken in the same way, I
should have considered him a plain, practical, earnest,
well-meaning man, who might be a master mechanic,
mariner, or man of business in any similar occupa-
tions.

I watched carefully not only every tone and
inflection of this voice, but the place from which it
seemed to come. It was not more than four feet from
me, in front of Mr. Ferguson, and not above a yard
from the floor. When the last word had been said,
and a candle lighted, Mr. Ferguson sat still with his
hands clasped together resting on his knees, and the
funnel was seen placed over them. It is very certain
that the funnel was brought from the table by some
force and volition not belonging to either of them, and
I am as certain as it is possible to be of any fact whatever that the voice, distinctly heard in a conversation
of ten or fifteen minutes' duration, was not that of
any one of the only five persons present.

On the first day of the New year, 1866, early

in the morning, I, in company with the Davenports and Mr. Fay, arrived in Dublin. On leaving the boat we went to an Inn on the quay to obtain some breakfast. We had not been long seated at the table before our spirit friends greeted our arrival with a shower of raps. We first sought Mr. Lauder who introduced us to Mr. I. Mc. Donnell. This gentleman I found knew but little of Spiritualism, but had been fighting the battle of mesmerism for several years, and is an earnest and intelligent advocate of other unpopular subjects. With the assistance of these gentlemen we established ourselves at the Queen's Arms Hotel Sackville Street, and made arrangements for giving a *Séance* there. For this purpose invitations were sent to the Press and several influential gentlemen, some of whom were connected with Trinity College. About forty attended. I commenced by asking them to dismiss from their minds, as much as possible, all they had heard, through rumour or the press, about the Davenports and to form an opinion from their own observation. I told them that on no subject that had come under my observation had there been a greater amount of falsehood and I was afraid wilful misrepresentation propagated by the press; —not only were the Davenports abused and misrepresented, but the public had been grossly abused and imposed upon by it. I said we came before them to submit facts on which every one was capable of exercising his faculties and forming his own judgment—that we offered no theories, and called upon them to indulge in or accept no fancies, but simply to witness a number of facts which would be put before them without mystery or disguise. I remarked that the fact of the cabinet being broken to pieces at Liverpool and Huddersfield was a proof there were no mechanical appliances about it. I alluded to the contest that had been going on with the conjurors, who at first boasted they could do all the Davenports did, but when challenged, declined on the ground that they had not had so much practice as the Brothers. I assured them that the Davenports owed nothing to practice, for at the age of twelve they possessed their extraordinary powers in full; and that had they chosen to come out in Europe as accomplished professors of legerdemain they would have carried the whole world with them and made a large fortune. I begged them to bear in mind that for twelve years before coming to Europe the Davenports had displayed their phenomena in every part of the United States, before the largest and most intelligent audiences. Judges, senators, the ablest and most practical lawyers, the acutest men of science, had seen them and examined their manifestations, and tested them by the most searching examination, and yet, neither in that country, in France nor England, had any-one been able to detect the slightest atom of fraud or delusion, and would never do so for the simple reason that it did not exist. I concluded my remarks by alluding to the wonderful phenomenon of matter passing through matter as demonstrated in the coat experiment, and calling upon scientific men to investigate these facts as the most important we were acquainted with.

My speech evidently had a good effect and increased the interest of my hearers, and one journal remarked of it that it was "free from the jargon of conjurers." The usual manifestations took place and were witnessed with astonishment and caused much speculation. A Mr. Trail, a man of note at Trinity College, entered the cabinet with the Brothers and on emerging from it exclaimed "That's grand by Jove." One of the Editors of the *Irish Times* also entered the cabinet and reported favourably of his experience. The Dark *Séance* followed and went off equally satisfactory. A profound impression was obviously made on the company which included two Rev. D. Ds., one of whom Rev. Dr. Tisdal offered his coat to be put on Mr Fay. This gentleman, considering his position, which was that of the most popular and fashionable clergyman in Dublin, acted a bold and manly part. He not only stood up for the facts, but proclaimed them far and wide, and wrote in the public papers in defence of the Davenports when their integrity was assailed. The next morning long and favourable notices appeared in all the papers and an excitement was created that for the time threw Fenianism into the shade. To convey an idea of the favourable impression produced by the first *Séance*, I give some extracts from the articles that appeared.

The "Freeman's Journal," after describing the phenomena witnessed, sums up thus—

"It would be perhaps, wearisome to go further into detail —suffice it to say that we witnessed the strangest and most unaccountable performance that could be thought of next to the sacred miracles. The Messrs. Davenport could not certainly have had assistance in the cabinet from any human being whatever. It is nothing but a thin shell of wood placed upon three trestles, and all who wished could watch every outside part of it during the whole night. During the dark part of the performance Messrs. Fay and Davenport sat on the same floor as the audience and within reach of almost a dozen of them. They certainly succeeded in astonishing all who had the pleasure of attending their soiree yesterday evening."

The "Irish Times" has the following sensible remarks to begin with—

"The Davenports, respecting whom so much has been written, have visited Dublin, and last evening held a séance in the Queen's Arms Hotel, upper Sackville Street. That they are possessed with mysterious power, bordering almost on the supernatural, would appear to be undoubted. The phenomena which they present astound the audience and defy all efforts at discovery. It is better to abstain from the expression of any decided opinion as to the agency employed in the manifestations, and simply relate what one has witnessed. Many opinions respecting them have been formed, and some of an adverse character urged with a degree of acerbity by the English press. Statements too have been made that their agency has been discovered, and that the manifestations produced were merely the efforts of successful conjurors. In that opinion few impartial persons can concur, and certainly, none who were present at the séance last evening. Mystery of the darkest description pervades the entire performance to such an extent that the sceptical were almost induced to abandon scepticism and join in the very extravagant and absurd opinion that the phenomena presented were the result of a supernatural agency.

"Saunder's Newsletter and Daily Advertiser" says of the first *Séance*—

"For three hours we were in an atmosphere so pervaded with mystery and wonder that long ere the performance was over we had given up all hope of finding the key to anything we saw."

The "Daily Express," equally bewildered, goes on to say—

"Much has been said and published of the surprising feats performed by these young men—and however prepared those present might have been to witness all that the most extravagant fancy could imagine—and notwithstanding the scepticism of many was openly expressed, the proceedings last evening eclipsed the anticipations of the most sanguine, staggered the prejudices of those the last to admit of supernatural agency, and evoked from all the most unequivocal and decided marks of approbation.

To account for these by ordinary laws of nature seems impossible ; that a supernatural agency should be invoked common sense forbade believing, and the audience while acknowledging the unaccountable nature of the means employed, were content to express their astonishment and give the Brothers every credit for candour and extraordinary ability."

It will be observed that, in all these articles, it was endeavoured to qualify the accounts by suggesting conjuring as an explanation. This was the error that the London Press fell into. Had the writers been content with simply reporting facts and abstained from offering a theory to account for them, their subsequent difficulty in the matter would have been avoided ; but having offered a theory at the onset they vainly endeavoured to bolster it by misrepresentation and unfairness. As an example, a letter appeared in the " Star " stating that a Mr. Dempster at Eastbourne, had detected Mr. Fay's hand in the cabinet. I wrote a letter in explanation but its insertion was refused. I then called upon the Editor and remonstrated with him on his unfair conduct, his reply was " We believe the Davenports to be impostors, for Tolmaque can do all they do, and we have determined to publish every thing we can against them and to admit nothing in their favour."

To render what I write more intelligible to such of my readers who have not witnessed the manifestations, I think it will be well to give a brief description of the *Séances*, and explain how they are conducted. Two gentlemen are first selected to act as a committee, their duties being to examine the cabinet and its properties, to tie the Brothers, to close the doors, to watch closely

the manifestations and to report to the audience
from time to time what takes place.   The method
of binding and the extent of rope are left to the
discretion of the committee.   The usual plan
adopted is to tie the wrists together behind the back ;
the cords are then placed through holes in the
seats and carried to the legs, round which they are
passed above the ankles ; the legs are also tied
above the knees, in such a way as to prevent any
lateral motion.   The instruments, consisting of a
guitar, tambourine, violin, horn and bells, are then
placed in the cabinet and the doors are closed ;
all the bolts, which are simple slip-bolts, being
inside, the last door that is closed can only be
fastened from the inside, which is immediately
done.   The horn will then be thrown out at the
hole in the centre door, and is frequently ejected
while the door is being shut.   After every manifestation an examination of the fastenings is made,
and in no instance is any alteration observable.
It consequently follows that if the Davenports
threw the horn out they must not only have
untied themselves but tied themselves in the
same manner, in the space of a few seconds.   The
bells will be rung at the window, and hands
appear of different sizes ; long, naked arms are
also protruded through it.   The violin is tuned
and played upon, the other instruments accom-
panying it.   During these proceedings the doors
are frequently thrown open and generally in the
midst of the noise, when the Brothers are always
found to be tied in the same manner as at first.
At length they are released from their bonds.
They again enter the cabinet with the ropes at
their feet. and in about three minutes are discovered bound hand and foot in a very skilful and

secure manner. The same kind of manifestations are then renewed, and one of the committee is allowed to enter the cabinet and sit between the brothers, resting a hand on each, so as to detect any motion if there were any. While thus seated the committee man will be manipulated by hands, and the instruments carried about and played around him. As a final test flour is placed in each hand of the Davenports, and whilst holding it the instruments will be played, clean hands exhibited and the complicated fastenings removed, and no mark of the flour is ever seen. The Davenports then come out of the cabinet and empty their hands of the flour before the company. This last experiment ought to be conclusive to every impartial and unprejudiced mind, for a little reflection must enable anyone, capable of judging of facts, to see the great improbability, not to say utter impossibility, of a person dressed in black cloth, being able to disengage himself from a series of knotted ligatures by his own agency without showing traces of the flour on his clothes, which is never the case with the Davenports. It is one of those things which no amount of practice would enable a person to accomplish; as well might we expect an acrobat by practice to maintain himself on a rope insufficiently strong to support him.

The dark *Séance* is conducted as follows. The company sit in chairs arranged in the form of a half circle, the ends of which join the wall so as to prevent any ingress. Those occupying the front seats are requested to join hands, which is a security against persons leaving their places during the intervals of darkness. A small table is placed within the semi-circle on which are placed two guitars, a tambourine, and bells.   Mr. Fay and Mr. Ira Davenport sit on either side of the table.   The light is then extinguished and a lashing of ropes is heard, also the guitars floating in the air.   On the production of a light the mediums are found with their hands behind them securely bound.   The light is again extinguished and the guitars are heard twanging and flying like birds in every direction and with great rapidity.   This experiment is repeated with the instruments illuminated with phosphorous, by the light of which their careering in the air is clearly seen.   To prove that the mediums do not move from their seats, paper is placed under their feet and their position marked upon it.

At the request of one of the company Mr. Fay's coat is taken from his back with the rapidity of thought,   and a light being struck at the moment the coat may be frequently seen in its flight upwards.   On an examination being immediately made, Mr. Fay's wrists are found to be tightly bound to the back of the chair.   A coat belonging to one of the company is then put on with the same marvellous rapidity as his own was taken off. The ropes are then unbound, the guitars at the same time sounding in the air, and as a concluding and conclusive experiment, two of the company are requested to hold Mr. Fay, and whilst he is held hand and foot the guitar is floated and played upon.

L ke the four test at the termination of the cabinet Séance, this test of holding Mr. Fay puts the matter beyond all doubt, for when a man is securely held he is disqualified from doing any act requiring the movement of his limbs.   The rest depends upon the good faith of those who hold him and the precautions taken against the cooperation of a confederate, and I need not say that these matters are well looked to by sharp and shrewd investigators.

It will be seen from the foregoing description of the two *Séances* that the principal use of the cabinet is to avoid placing the audience in darkness by providing the condition of darkness necessary for the production of the manifestations. Darkness, if not a condition absolutely necessary, is one that favours the phenomena. Why it is so has never been satisfactorily explained. For the first few years of their mediumship the Davenports obtained their manifestations only in the dark *Séance* form, and it was, that the hands which were felt in the dark, might be seen in the light, that the cabinet was devised. It was at first a mere box with a hole in it, and its only use was, as I have intimated, to enable the spirits to show their hands. A Mr. Lewis, residing at Dublin, who knew the Davenports as boys at Buffalo, told me he was present the first night a cabinet exhibition took place. In a letter to the *Irish Times* he says "the statements of your correspondents are not borne out by *my experience* extending over a period of fifteen years. The Brothers Davenport were then known to me as boys at school, yet more astounding demonstrations then occurred in their presence than those which have been witnessed in Dublin. At that time they were beneath the claim to praise now so lavishly heaped on them of "expert conjurors," for they were only children and exhibited their phenomena to please their friends and to satisfy and dissatisfy others, very much like the present time barring the charge at the doors."

The *Séances* continued to be held in the Queen's Arms Hotel for about a week when, in consequence of a letter calling on us to give the public an opportunity of witnessing the exhibition, we decided on removing to the Antient Concert Rooms. This new series of *Séances* was well attended and the people were well behaved and courteous. A lively controversy was kept up in the newspapers, and during the first fortnight it was no uncommon thing to see a dozen letters, for and against, in the *Irish Times* of a morning. Then there was a conjuror, Dr. Lynn (his real name is Symonds) who had a cabinet and did the "rope trick"— this exposer of the " humbug of Spiritualism " took part in the discussion ; while a rival conjuror asserted that Dr. Lynn could not do what the Davenports did, neither could any other conjuror. A correspondent under the name of *Medicus* published a challenge but it was of such a preposterous nature that it was evident he knew nothing of the subject, and I replied to him to the effect that he had better make himself acquainted with the nature of the exhibition before sending challenges, and that we were not in Dublin either to give or accept challenges but to exhibit facts.

Thus matters went on very swimmingly for about a fortnight when a circumstance occurred of a most unexpected and inexplicable nature, which to this day I have never been able to account for, so far as the conduct of the principal actor is concerned.

On one evening during the dark *Séance* just as Mr. Fay's coat was about to be removed, a match was struck but not ignited, which emitted sufficient light for objects, for the moment, to be clearly seen. I protested against the striking of a light as contrary to the conditions, begged it might not be repeated, and thought no more of the matter. Judge then of my surprise the next morning, when Mr. Lauder, in company with a Mr. Robinson came to us with very long faces and expressed a wish to speak to us in private. They said they had a very serious accusation to make, which was that Mr. Lauder had observed Ira Davenport out of his place when the light was struck the night before. I expressed my suprise and told him he must be mistaken, for I was sitting close behind and saw him sitting quietly in the chair. Nothing, he said, would convince him to the contrary, and it was proposed to test the Davenports then and there. The room was accordingly darkened and some musical instruments procured. I was requested to leave the room, which I protested against, alleging that as it was a test *Séance*, I ought to be allowed to witness fair play on the part of the Davenports; but they still persisted that I should leave the room. I told them I would take my position between them on the sofa and that they might hold me. No, they would not be satisfied with anything that took place while I was in the room and almost in plain terms intimated that we were all swindlers and that I was the biggest. I appealed to the Davenports as to how I should act; they said I had better leave, and accordingly I did so. In about half-an-hour the *Séance* terminated, and I was then informed that no manifestations could be obtained. It was then arranged, contrary to my wish, to try again the next morning. In the course of the day Mr. Fay said to me " I don't like the idea of being humbugged about by that Lauder, let us go and hear what John says," and forthwith I and Fay started

off to the Antient Concert Rooms and got into the
cabinet. The doors were hardly closed when the
horn was heard in motion and Kate's shrill voice
speaking through it. " We have come to talk to
you about this affair with Lauder," Fay said.
Oh, John must come and talk to you about that.
The next minute John's voice was heard saluting
us like any mortal visitor. I said, " How was it
you did not give any manifestations this morning
—weren't you present, or weren't the conditions
right?" *That was'nt it : they insulted you,
Cooper, that's why we would not give any manifestations.
You have arranged to go to them to morrow, but don't
do so. Write to Lauder and tell him that the Brothers
are under a contract with you, and tell him that in consequence of the manner in which he acted towards you
this morning, you will not allow the proposed Séance to
take place : but don't tell him I told you.*

Mr Lauder had threatened to publish his accusation in the newspapers, which, with the subsequent failure of the *Séance,* I considered might be
very damaging to the Davenports and the cause I
sought to promote, inasmuch as his letter would
only too readily be copied by the English press,
whilst any statements I might make by way of
explanation would receive no notice whatever. I
was therefore anxious, if possible, to prevent him
adopting the course he threatened, and endeavoured
to conciliate him by proposing a test *Séance,* to
take place before a number of qualified gentlemen
whose testimony would have weight with the public ; the advice of John therefore took me by surprise. It seemed like taking the bull by the
horns and defying Mr. Lauder to do his worst. I
wrote the letter in accordance with the instructions
of " John," and in due course appeared a letter

from Mr. Lauder making the charge against Ira Davenport, and also a letter of a half-apologetic character from Mr. Robinson regretting that he had ever been favourably disposed towards the Davenports. Both these gentlemen were in a very awkward position ;—Mr. Lauder for having been instrumental in getting the Davenports to Dublin, and, when there, doing all he could to establish them in public favour ; and Mr. Robinson for having a few days before written a letter to the *Irish Times* fully endorsing the genuineness of the manifestations. In this letter he says, " During the dark *Séance* the motion of the musical instruments through the air is most astonishing. This could not be accomplished either by strings, wires or any other mechanical contrivance, and I may mention that while witnessing this part of the exhibition in London, some person suddenly lighted a wax-match, hoping to discover the trick, but instead of making any discovery the Messrs. Davenport and Fay were seen tightly bound in their chairs, and the musical instruments were falling to the ground."

" Viewing all these matters, I have come to the conclusion that the phenomena are of a most extraordinary character, that they cannot be produced by any mechanical or physical means, and consequently that the Davenports possess a power which we do not understand."

Six days after writing this, Mr. Robinson expresses his opinion that " All their performances are merely the result of long and acquired practice, aided by their own conditions and darkness " and concludes by saying " I rather regret having, on a former occasion, expressed a somewhat different opinion, the result of my first crude observa-

tions ; but had I not acted as I did, I could not
have had the opportuuty of so thoroughly investi-
gating the matter, and so fully exposing their delusion to the public ".

Mr. Lauder in his letter says " Should the
Davenports attempt to continue their exhibition,
and represent their sleight-of-hand tricks as the
result of occult or preternatural agency, they can
be always detected in their dark *Séance* by having
a darkened lantern in readiness which can be
rapidly flashed—a match being too slow for these
expert operators."

But alas ; for Mr. Lauder, his positive assurance
that the Davenports "could always be detected"
by the employment of a dark lantern was proved
to be a fallacy, and by Mr. Robinson, who not
satisfied with seeing a match struck in London,
sent his son with a lantern, and in the course
of the *Séance* flashed the light on the mediums,
who were discovered seated quietly in their chairs
and " the instruments falling to the ground."

In reply to Messrs. Lauder and Robinson I
wrote a letter which is too long for reproduction
here. In it I commented on the inconsistent conduct of these gentlemen and said it was an ex-
emplification of the saying "Save me from my
friends," and asked " Is it reasonable to suppose
that nobody among the hundred persons present
have seen the delinquent but Mr. Lauder ?" and,
by way of addenda, I published the following
letters from five gentlemen all well known in Dublin
and esteemed for their worth and honour. The
first is the Rev. Dr. Tisdal of whom I have already spoken. Mr. Armstrong is a Solicitor.
Mr. Farrall a veterinary surgeon. Mr. Fitzgerald
a Magistrate and Deputy Lieutenant, and Mr.

Lewis a lithographer. Such testimony ought to settle the matter for ever. I may add that I have been present, at least a score of times, when a light has been struck, but nothing was discovered except perhaps the folly of those who forfeited their honour in attempting to find out the secret.

On the evening of last monday. the 15th. I was present at one of the dark Séances given by the Messrs. Davenport. A light was suddenly struck by one of the audience. I saw Mr. Ira Davenport and Mr. Fay seated as before the darkness was produced, and remarked to the gentleman who accompanied me to witness the results, and sat next me, with his hand in mine, that the unexpected production of the light had, at all events afforded no discernable evidence that Mr. Davenport and Mr. Fay moved from their seats. My impression then was, and is still, that the striking of the light was an instance of complete failure in the effort to detect motion upon the part of Messrs. Davenport and Fay. The coat of the latter was on before the light was extinguished, and when the match was struck the coat was off, and visibly descending upon the floor.

To the proof of the foregoing statement I can bear testimony.

C. E. TISDALL.

January 18, 1866.

———

When, at Monday evening's séance, the light was suddenly, and as I said at the time, unfairly struck by one of the audience, insamuch as it was contrary to the condition of the séance, Mr. Davenport and Mr. Fay were sitting tied in their chairs. I watched closely, and they did not appear to have moved. My friend and I were sitting within a few yards of Mr. Fay.

The sudden production of the light seems to me to have totally failed in detecting any movement on the part of either of those gentlemen, as the friend sitting next me, in whose hand mine was at the time, remarked, there was no evidence whatever of either Mr. Fay or Mr. Davenport having stirred from their places.

JOHN ARMSTRONG.

45, Lower Dominick-street, Jan. 18, 1866.

To Messrs Davenport and Fay.

Dublin, 18th January. 1866.

Gentlemen,—Seeing letters in the " Irish Times " of this morning referring to your séance of Monday night last, the 15th inst., and stating that when a match had been ignited, that Mr. Davenport was seen away some distance from the chair on which he had been previously seated. In justice to you. I wish to observe that I, with some other friends who were seated in the front row, and within a few feet of those who were manifesting the usual phenomena, saw not the least movement in the case of those who were then performing, 'Tis quite true a match was ignited, and, insufficient as the light was, it afforded those sitting in front the full opportunity of observing that those parties manifesting the phenomena were seen in the same position as that in which they had been previous to the light being turned off.—I am, gentlemen your obedient servant,   J. J. FARRALL.

———

Out of evil comes good, and the result of this Irish *exposé*, which, as I anticipated, was published in the English papers without my reply, was to strengthen the favourable impression that had been produced, and, the interest excited, to give addtiional publicity to the subject. As the spirits afterwards remarked to me in reference to the exposure in America of a counterfeit medium —a young girl who was detected in having secreted things about her person, that even an affair of that kind did good, because it drew public attention to the subject,—anything, they said, that caused the subject to be agitated, whether favour able or unfavourable, benefited Spiritualism " because it was true."   Although one *Séance* is for the most part a counterpart of another still incidents frequently occur to vary the proceedings and give additional interest. Sometimes these incidents are of an amusing character. I will mention a few that happened in Dublin.

At one of our early *Séances* we experienced great

annoyance from an Englishman, who kept calling out " humbug," and words of a similar meaning. He at length impugned the honour of the committee, who were military officers. Asking my permission, they got down from the platform, and took the offender by the collar, and walked him out of the room, to the great satisfaction of the audience.

On another occasion, in consequence of a guitar resting twice on the lap of a gentleman occupying a seat in the front row, some remarks were made by a person behind, implying confederacy. This roused the blood of the Irishman, who forthwith began by saying, " Do you know who I am? I am the editor of," &c. and insisted upon the accuser exchanging seats with him.

By the adoption of the balloting system, we were on the whole, fortunate in obtaining good and fair committee men. On one occasion, however, we had a person, named Simington, a photographer (our principal opponents have been photographers,) who adopted the Hulley and Cummins tactics He operated on William Davenport, who very soon began to complain of the brutality of the tying. I asked if there was a medical man present who would examine the cords. Immediately an old gentleman stepped on the platform, and at once began by assuring the audience that he was in no way prejudiced. He examined the wrists, and said he could get his finger in. I then began to fear trouble. William Davenport still complained of the pain, and had yet to undergo the process of having his legs bound. I advised him to bear the pain if possible, knowing, that if I could but get the doors closed, he would soon be released. This was at length accomplished, and the efforts were at once directed to liberating the medium, which took about ten minutes, during which time but few manifestations took place. Mr. S— urged this against us. On the Brothers being re-tied, Mr. S— said they were not tied with a knot, but with a twist. To satisfy him that such was not the case we had the ropes untied and he acknowledged he was wrong. Finding himself defeated on all points he stood sulkily in a corner of the platform, and would neither retire nor take further part in the proceedings. This affair, was within an ace of being a repetition of the Leeds affair. The doctor who felt the wrists evidently put his finger into the rope that encircled both wrists. It resulted in triumph to the Davenports, and the feeling was strong against Mr. Simington and his partizans.

On one occasion a gentleman entered the cabinet without invitation from the Brothers. He pulled the doors to and then began to show his hand at the window, and afterwards grinned through it at the audience. He very soon begged to be let out, and came forth looking very pale and woe-begone, holding his hand to his head, having received some severe blows. His scepticism appeared to have been put to flight by the *striking* evidence he had received that there is something in creation besides matter. The next evening one of the committee entered the cabinet in the usual manner. He very soon began to beg to be let out. He complained of being struck on the head. I told him he was the first I knew of who had complained of rough treatment. I told him also that he was the first I had seen wear a hat in the cabinet, which might have had something to do with it. There had evidently been an attempt to bonnet the gentleman as it is vulgarly called.

Sometimes when persons enter the cabinet and sit with the Brothers strange freaks will be practised on them. Their neckerchief will be taken off, the breast pin removed and stuck into the coat behind, and if spectacles happen to be worn they will be transferred to the face of one of the Davenports. When Mr. Coleman entered the cabinet in London, his handkerchief was taken from his pocket and tied over his head. I have, at different times, seen at least three hundred persons enter the cabinet, all of whom certified there was no movement on the part of the Brothers.

While at Dublin we had occasional visits from the spirits in private. Sometimes while seated at dinner with the mediums. I would observe a gentle tapping on my knee which was followed by a grasp as of a large powerful hand taking hold of my limb, and often too vigorous to be agreeable. The Davenports would also have the same kind of experience, and sometimes they would be constrained to remonstrate with the spirits on account of their rough treatment, and in one or two instances, left the table to avoid it. Raps would be heard and sometimes loud reports as if the table were struck with a hammer. In addition to feeling hands underneath the table, they might occasionally be seen protruding under the cloth, and on two or three occasions, in answer to Mr. Fay's question " Can you lift the table John ? " the table was raised in the air with all the dinner things on it. All this took place in the light and nobody present but ourselves. The table, I may observe, was a square dining table about four feet square, of considerable weight. Once during these unsought and unlooked for manifestations my bread lying beside my place suddenly sprung into the air. This is about the extent of my experiences with the Davenports in the light, but I had others in the dark which I shall allude to in due course.

I frequently made suggestions to the spirits with a view to vary and improve the *Séances* and to render the experiments more conclusive, but I found them for the most part opposed to anything in the shape of innovation. They would however give their reasons for not adopting my suggestions and I generally found there was wisdom in their conclusions. Once in reply to a suggestion to do something still more extraordinary they said *"People can't believe what they see now—There was a man last night frightened and left the room. No, we can't make any alterations—at any rate at present. It depends more upon the state of the mind of those who see these things than what we do; some men can't believe their own senses"* However, they acquiesced in one of my suggestions. I said " you make so much drumming noise when you play the instruments that the violin can scarcely be heard. I think if you were to play a slow tune and not make so much noise with the other instruments it would have a good effect." This hint was taken and at night a tune was played differing in style to any thing I had heard before, and the time was softly beat on the tambourine. This tune I have since ascertained to be " Washington's March over the Delaware," and it has been played at every subsequent *Séance*. During the time we were in Ireland there was a great variety in the tunes played, sometimes Irish and Scotch melodies, and once " Yankee Doodle " was played, the speed increasing at every repetition until the tune was hardly distinguishable.

After exhibiting for three weeks in Dublin we left that city and visited Cork. Just as the railway enters this town there is a tunnel. Whilst passing through it I felt something tapping me on the head. I then heard a voice which was rendered indistinct by the noise of the carriages, and I consequently took no notice of it till Ira Davenport said " Cooper, there's Kate calling you." The voice then spoke loud enough to be heard above the rattle of the train, which was now going at a slow rate. It said, *You must be careful what you say in this place—they are queer people here—say nothing about Spiritualism. Be firm—you are not firm enough; don't give into them.*

I then said "shall I put it upon a scientific basis?"

Put it on no basis at all—let the facts speak for themselves; the less that's said the better.

I told Kate her wishes should be complied with, and the next minute we were at the station. It will not be worth while to enter into the particulars of the *Séances* at Cork. We remained there a week, during which time the exhibition was witnessed by most of the principal inhabitants. Everything passed off satisfactorily, and a profound impression was obviously made. In this town I observed less scepticism than in any, before or subsequently, visited. After visiting Limerick and Waterford (where a gentleman called and desired the Davenports for his satisfaction to take a " Bible oath " that they were passive agents) we returned to Dublin, intending to exhibit at the Rotunda, and then, either to visit other towns in Ireland, or to go to Scotland. On the Day we arrived at Dublin, Fay said to me "John wants to speak

to you, he came to me after I got to bed last night."
In accordance therefore with the expressed wish
of "John" we went to a bedroom, and darkened
it by nailing a rug before the windows, a matter
of no little difficulty. When this was nearly done
Kate said, *There, that will do—that's dark enough.*
We then took our seats in a corner of the room,
having extemporised a horn by rolling a piece of
music into a cone and tying it with string. This
was laid on the bed. John's husky voice was
soon heard speaking through it, and proceeded
to tell me what to say to the audience at night.
He then said, *Cooper, I want you to go to Russia
with the Brothers; you have done a good work in
this country, but it is no use stopping any longer—get
on to Scotland as fast as you can and then go straight
away to Russia.* The voice ceased and the paper
horn was thrown across the room.

I have frequently noticed that "John" is very
short and concise in his conversation, and by no
means disposed to be communicative. He rarely
condescends to talk upon subjects that have no
connection with his mission, and always speaks
at once to the point, his utterances indicating great
earnestness of purpose. He is what might be
called a man of few words. Kate once said, *You
will be surprised when you see John what a great
man he is; he possesses wonderful will power.* He
always has an answer ready, but sometimes
hesitates to find the right word in conversation.
At times he is witty and I have even known him
make a joke. Ira and I got into the cabinet one
day after the *Séance* was over, when Ira said "You
gave me a precious rap on the head just now."
John's ready answer was, *It wasn't me, it was the
trumpet.* Kate, too, attempts to be witty at times.

She was asked (I was not present at the time), whether she and John ever quarrelled, to which she replied, *O yes, we are married you know.* Unlike John, Kate will talk any length of time, as long in fact as she can find anything to talk about, even if it be the most frivolous nonsense; but I must do her the justice to say that she talks sensibly enough at times, and I have heard great wisdom in her utterances, and satisfactory answers given to profound philosophical questions.

On our return to Dublin a letter appeared in the *Irish Times* calling on those, who had boasted so much of their ability to discover the secret, to make good their assertions, saying it was evident the Davenports did not shirk investigation. This put some of these knowing ones on their mettle, and desperate attempts were in consequence made to fathom the mystery by striking lights, putting black on the hands of the mediums unknown to them, and other cunning devices, but all to no purpose; notwithstanding all these attempts to "find out the trick," they were just as far off as ever. The man who had charge of the hall told me that numbers of persons had been to him to ask if he could throw any light on the matter, which he confessed he was unable to do, but told them they might examine the cabinet. As a last resource Dr. Lynn, the conjuror, came to the rescue, and announced a lecture in which he undertook to expose Spiritualism thoroughly. This, of course, like all conjurors' tricks was a mere device for getting money. The result of this lecture I do not know, for my career in Dublin was unexpectedly brought to a close some two or three days earlier than it was intended, the particulars respecting which I will proceed to state.

I have already spoken of establishing a paper in the interest of Spiritualism. This was published at the Spiritual Lyceum, London; and both the institution and paper were under the management of Mr. Powell. Just before I left London Mr. Sothern, the actor, addressed a letter to the *Glasgow Citizen* in reply to a statement in the *Spiritual Magazine*, to the effect that Mr. Sothern was formerly a member of a spiritual society in America, known as the Miracle Circle, and that Mr. Sothern acted as medium. Mr. Sothern in his letter admitted the existence of the " Circle " and his connection with it, but denied the spiritual origin of the manifestations that were produced, and stated that he had systematically hoaxed the public for two years for his amusement, and concluded by stigmatising " every Spiritualist as either an impostor or idiot, and every Spiritualist exhibitor who made money by his exhibition as a swindler;" and asserted his ability to " do all that they can do and more." In reply to which, I addressed a letter to the *Glasgow Citizen*, the substance of which was that as Mr. Sothern had asserted that " he had done and could do all the Davenports did and more," if he would satisfactorily explain the *modus operandi* by which the Davenport manifestations were produced, I would give one hundred guineas to the Dramatic College. Mr. Sothern took no notice of the letter. This is all I had personally to do with Mr Sothern.

The Sothern letter reached America and attracted the attention of Col. Du Solle, Editor of the *New York Sunday Times*, who was acquainted with the whole proceedings and knew Mr. Sothern very well. He wrote an article on the 'subject in his paper and mentioned facts that did not reflect favourably on Mr. Sothern's private character. The paper containing Col. Du Solle's article was brought to the Spiritual Lyceum by an American gentleman, and Mr. Powell incautiously gave it insertion in the *Spiritual Times*. Of the whole matter I was entirely ignorant, and almost the first I heard of it was on reading in the *Irish Times* a report of the proceedings at the Police Court in London, and that a warrant had been issued for my apprehension to answer a charge of libel. The same evening at the conclusion of the dark *Séance* a policeman took me in charge and conveyed me to a police station preparatory to taking me to London the next morning. I wrote the following account, at the time, of my experience under the title of

Three Nights in the Police Cell.

I AM about to give, or rather attempt to give, a simple account of my premature and unexpected return from Dublin, and my incarceration in the police cell; and had I the practised hand of the writer of "A Night in a Workhouse," my experience might be as interesting to the public as that world-known narrative. Lacking this ability, a narrative of the following facts will doubtless be read with interest by my friends, independent of any sympathy they may have for the principal actor in the three nights' drama. The hero of the Casual Ward was an amateur. My sufferings, though not like his, self-imposed, were equally unmerited:—

At the instance of Mr. Sothern I was arrested by a police officer at the conclusion of a Davenport Seance, at the Dublin Rotunda—fortunately the last but one in Dublin. I proceeded with the officer to the hotel to collect my luggage, where I took some tea. I was next conveyed in a cab to a Police Station. This was about eleven o'clock at night. Here I was conducted

into a white-washed room, on the side of which were
doors with little grated openings. These I afterwards
discovered to be cells, in which offenders are temporarily
confined. There was a fire in the room, at each side of
which were forms, on which sat two or three policemen.
The first object that arrested my attention on entering
this place was a woman's face at the barred opening of
one of the cells. This face was of an ashy paleness, and
made grimaces, and uttered very hideous noises. In
a little time the utterances became articulated, and an
appeal to be let out for warmth was clearly heard, and
persistively repeated. At first the appeal was met by
a threat to exclude the light if she did not leave off ;
but after the application became more moderate, she
was promised a five minutes' warmth at the fire. The
bolts were drawn, the door opened, and out came a
fine young woman, very dirtily dressed, who at once
proceeded to take off her shoes and stockings, and dry
them by the fire. After sitting a few minutes she was
told she had been there long enough, and was again
locked in the cell, when after a few remonstrances and
complaints she became quiet. In the room were two
benches, on one of which lay a poor miserable object,
in the form of a man, to whom I shall presently refer.
It was intimated that I could lie down on the other.
I did so, making use of my portmanteau for a pillow.
I had not been reclining long, when the Brothers
Davenport called in to take another farewell. Allusion was made to their incarceration in Oswego Gaol,
and they gave an account of the opening of the prison
doors by the spirits. This naturally excited the
attention of the big policemen (they were all over six
feet, and appeared to be selected for their size, like the
body guard of Frederick the Great), and I need not
say they looked very incredulous. The Davenports
also said that their prison was a much worse place,
that they had to suspend their bed by ropes from the
ceiling to keep clear of vermin. The Brothers also
spoke of the kindness of friends, the number of visits
they received, the quantity of good things they had
brought them, that altogether, they somewhat regretted

when the term of imprisonment had expired. This visit ended, I lay down again, and got into a doze, when a fresh arrival disturbed my partial slumbers. It was a woman, or what was called a woman, in a dreadful state of intoxication. She wanted to go to the fire. Her wish was opposed, and she made an effort to go there by force, which was resisted by the great policemen, who, without any parleying, each taking hold of an arm, dragged her to the cell, and closed the door against her, as she vainly essayed to force her way out as it was being closed. Then began a storm of human rage such as I had never heard before, and could not have conceived possible. The iron door was frantically struck by the closed fists of the desperate wretch in her vain effort. A continuous howl, a mixture of rage and despair, through which an occasional articulate word could be heard, was kept up. Presently the wild howling relapsed into articulate cursing. She swore by all the saints in heaven and devils in hell. For five minutes, at least, her objurgations were made in the name of the Holy Ghost. "Let me out to warm myself. Give me a ha'porth of fire. My mother never brought me up to be a ———. If a woman comes here with fine clothes, you do not treat her so. If it was not for such as me, you would not have such a good coat on your back." Such were the kind of utterances she gave forth, as soon as her rage allowed her to speak, to all of which the policemen were perfectly indifferent. They took but little notice of her, except to say now and then as they paced the room, "You shall have a ha'porth of fire when you are quiet." They said but little, knowing from experience that anything they could say would not avail in arresting the torrent of mad passions, but would only stimulate it. At one time she was threatened with having the little barred window closed up, so as to render the cell dark. This threat succeeded for a time in quelling the frantic noise, but a fresh outbreak caused the threat to be put in force, and increased for a time the wretch's cries and curses. I feel sure that had they allowed the poor creature to sit a short time by the fire, when she first came in, this dreadful scene would have been avoided. In process of time the noise ceased, and once more asking for a "ha'porth of fire," she was allowed to come out and warm herself. And then was brought in a poor old woman. What her offence was did not transpire. Probably she was homeless. She was conducted to a cell without uttering a word or murmur. There were some more arrivals not calling for special notice.

About four o'clock, as I lay on my bench, I found the man who occupied the other bench had arisen and was seated by the fire adjusting his rags, one of the women looking through the bars volunteering to render him assistance with a needle. I looked up and saw he was a close-cropped, bullet-headed vagrant, who, from his appearance, had not long been out of prison. He was called by the policeman "Paddy," and judging from the conversation, appeared to be a "character," and "well known to the police ; " one of those waifs and strays of society, whose life is passed between the gaol, the workhouse, and the public-house. He was seated among his custodians telling them tales ; and as soon as he had finished one, was asked to "give us another tale, Paddy." I arose and was addressed by Paddy as "Doctor," and was asked my advice for his swelled throat.

At half-past five my policeman, in plain clothes, made his appearance, and announced that it was time to start. I had no other preparation to make than to put on my hat and take up my portmanteau, and was at his disposal ; I thanked the police for the night's lodging they had afforded me, bade them "Good Morning," and was taken in a cab to the railway station, and thence to the steam boat at Kingston. The morning was cold, the wind was biting, and the sea rough. During the passage my custodian came to me in my prostrate condition and charitably administered a little brandy. He was a good-natured, simple-minded man, and behaved very well to me ; and I understand he reported that I had behaved very well to him.

We were conveyed per Holyhead to London, nearly 300 miles in six hours, and arrived at our destination (the Police-station, in John Street, Edgeware Road), about seven. Here my name and address and offence were entered in a book, and I was conducted to a cell similar to those I had seen in Dublin. There were three of these cells in a row, with a passage along the front, the middle one of the three being allotted to me. It was a place about eight feet long by six feet broad, built of brick, with a saw-dust covered floor. It was fitted with a broad seat running along the back and one side, ending in a water-closet. This was the only furniture it contained. In the centre of the door was a little opening covered by a perforated piece of metal arranged to slide up and down. A gas-light from the passage shone through the holes of this window, by the light of which I was enabled to read; but to do so I had to shift the paper, so as to cause the light to run along the lines. This reading under difficulties was at length removed by the inspector ordering the slide to be let down. About ten I lay down for the night on my hard bed, but it was not long before I was disturbed by the unlocking of doors, and the flashing of a bull's-eye lantern, and by the inquiry if all was right, to which I had to answer. This process was gone through every hour of the night, and would be anything but pleasant to a sound sleeper. There were two or three fresh arrivals during the night, which were attended by some noise, but nothing like I had experienced in Dublin. I was assured that I had been greatly favoured, as it was the quietest Saturday night they had had for a long while. I dreaded more than anything having another prisoner put in my cell. Early in the morning I heard a man's voice and a boy's in the cell on my right, and a considerable moaning on my left. About eight o'clock I was informed that I could have what I liked brought from a neighbouring coffee-house, but nothing stronger than tea, and I ordered my breakfast accordingly. My neighbours were also asked whether they wanted any breakfast. Had they any money? The man said he had fourpence, and ordered provisions to the full amount. He was advised not to spend all at once as it was a long time till to-morrow morning. He de-cided, after some deliberation, on spending only threepence. The boy said he had also fourpence, and would like a cup of coffee and four slices of bread and butter. The policeman was astonished at such a large supply being wanted for so small a boy. The boy, however, said he would spend his fourpence all at once. "Well, growing boys do want as much to eat as men," was the answer; but the growing boy got nothing more till the next day. He asked for a little 'baccer,' and was told that birch would be more suita-ble for him.

In the course of the day I managed to ascertain that my neighbours on my right were a man and two boys. The man was in for begging and the boys for exhibiting white mice. Their conversation showed them to be professional beggars. In the other cell were three women whose offence was drunkenness. All the first part of this Sunday (it was a glorious Sunday as I could see by a stream of sunlight that shot across the passage, and once actually found its way into my cell), I heard but little of my female neighbours; they had not recovered from their last night's debauch—an occasional yawn was all I heard of them. They were asked if they wanted anything to eat. They said they had no money, and were consequently without food till the next morning, when they were provided with some. One of the police was a pious character; he administered a little advice to the prisoners, reminding them where the broad road led to, and expressed his sorrow that they still persisted in walking in it. He was evidently a member of some little Zion, and judging from his familiarity with Scripture, and the readiness with which he met every argument with a text, I have no doubt he occasionally officiated as preacher to the congregation of which he was a mem-ber. We got into conversation about Spiritualism, but everything I advanced was met with a text. However, I succeeded in interesting him, and he was anxious for further information. I also spoke to one of the inspectors on the subject.

At noon Mr. W. came to consult and console. His visit was like the gleam of sunlight that had before entered my cell.

In the afternoon the females, having revived, began to talk among themselves, and at length opened up a conversation with the prisoners on the other side of me. Presently I was saluted with the familiar sound of raps on my wall, and was asked what I was in for ? As I had but a dim idea of it, I could not give them much information. The "jolly beggars" now began singing, and in this way passed an hour or so merrily. The man was evidently a jovial companion, who could entertain his pot-house friends with a song when called upon. His favourite song was "The Low-Back'd Car." The boys also sang, and were well-up in the popular songs of the day. "Good-bye Sweetheart" and "Here we are again" (not an inappropriate one) were the style of songs they delighted in ; and when they were tired of singing, or had exhausted their *répertoire*, would whistle the "Mabel Waltz," and other popular melodies. One of the boys had an excellent idea of music, and with proper attention would make a good musician. I must do my companions in distress the justice to say, that I never heard anything immoral while I had the pleasure of their society.

In the midst of the singing the policeman enters and all is quiet. He opens the cell and enquires if all is right, and finds " all serene.' He looks in upon me and then goes to the next cell, saying, "Now, then, ladies, is there anything I can do for you ?" A conversation ensues ; policeman retires, and I am again saluted by raps, and am asked a question I cannot, in consequence of the Scotch brogue of the speaker, catch. My neighbour, the " jolly beggar,'' answers. " I do not mean you, I mean the gentleman in the next cell." The Scotch voice proceeded to inform me that she had ascertained what I was in for. She was entered "drunk and disorderly,' and I was in for "a bad libel." She asked me if she made much noise when she came in. I said I heard a great noise in the night.

Have you been often here ? I asked.

Yes a good many times.

I wonder you don't take warning from this.

I can't help it. They treated me to some whiskey, and my old man takes no account of me.

Does your husband know where you are ?

No, and would'nt care if he did.

What punishment do you expect to get ?

That depends on who the Magistrate is. Mr. Yardley lets us off with seven days. The others give us a month.

Do they give you anything to do?

Yes, pick oakum.

Well, I think you pay dearly for a little pleasure. I advise you not to do it again.

I am afraid I shall though.

She now began to question me.

Where did they take you ?

In Dublin.

Is that where you live ?

No. I have not been home for two months.

Have you a wife ?

No ; but I have five children.

Poor things, I hope they are taken care of.

They have to take care of themselves at present.

Do they know you are here ?

I don't think they do.

This colloquy, which helped to beguile the time, is sufficient to show that, degraded as the poor creature was, there were gleams of goodness in her nature.

She asked if I had a newspaper, and if there was any particular news in it. I looked to see if there were any murders, robberies, or suicides, and finding nothing very striking in that department, told her there was no news of importance. I thought it would be of no use telling her that the Habeas Corpus was about to be suspended.

The remainder of the day was spent in reading, and

reflecting, and writing with a pencil a short lecture which I now find difficult to decipher.

The night came, and the prisoners began to come in. I dreaded every fresh arrival, lest one should be put in my cell. Fortunately this did not occur. In the morning the beggars grumbled among themselves about lying on each other. Not being able to adjust themselves, they saluted the early morn with the songs they had sung the day before. At length the wished for hour of ten arrived. The prisoners were taken from their cells to the courtyard, when they went through the process of standing in a row, and answering to their names. I was left in my cell. My female friend, as she passed along the passage, looked at my window, and gave a smile of friendly recognition, and I saw by that glance, that sunken as this poor creature was, the "woman" was still there.

I thanked the police for their kindness to me, was conducted in a cab to the Police Court, and soon found myself in the presence of the great and impartial administrator of justice, the magnate of the Police Court. I there heard, for the first time, and rather to my astonishment, what a bad character I was, what a dreadful crime I had committed, that the libel was concocted by me in my office, and that I was captured in the theatre in Dublin. I was committed for trial at the Old Bailey for an offence I knew nothing of till I read, in an Irish paper, that a warrant was granted for my arrest.

I was at liberty again, and in the streets of London; but my mind was bewildered and as befogged as the black air I breathed. One street seemed as another to me; all seemed alike. In the evening I heard Emma Hardinge. She discoursed most eloquently on "Mystery," a fit subject, for everything seemed a mystery to me, even the kindness and consideration of so many friends. Miss Hardinge was said to excel herself on that occasion. Of that I know not; I only know she excelled everybody else I had ever heard. I would fain have addressed a few words to the meeting, in return for their expression of kindness and sympathy, but could not do so ;—my head was in a maze. I could not collect my thoughts, and was compelled to let my silence be the expression of my overburdened heart.

After these experiences in the Police cell, I hoped to be treated by the *free press* of England at least as an innocent man until I was proved guilty. The magistrate, Mr. Knox—before whom I was placed, gave me some rough *knocks*, entirely pre-judging my case. The "Daily Telegraph," assu-ming its own immaculate purity, in a leader introduced this choice sentence :—

"The proper punishment is that the offender should be hauled to the bar with a policeman's hand on his collar. Other and more serious penalties may have to be inflicted afterwards, but the first thing to do is to stamp and brand the libeller, to fix upon him the stigma of disgrace."

I wrote an explanatory letter couched in res-pectful language to the " Daily Telegraph," but of course the letter did not appear. And yet, the " Daily Telegraph " is a *liberal* journal !

The Davenports then went to Belfast and thence to Edinburgh and Glasgow, where they were very successful, especially in the former of the two places. Mr. M'Donnell, of whom I have spoken, acted as my substitute at Belfast. On his return to Dublin, Mr. Lauder said to him, " Well, did you find out the rogues ?" " Yes, and the fools too," was the reply !

Mr. Sothern and the Davenports were at Glas-gow at the same time, when a letter in one of the local papers called his attention to my challenge. He, however, thought " discretion to be the better part of valour," and took no notice of it.

The Davenports then came to London, when there was of course more said in the papers about the "irrepressible Davenports." They exhibited at the Hanover Square Rooms for a week under my superintendence, but the audiences not being sufficiently good to justify their remaining in London, it was determined to consult John, with reference to the future, who tendered his counsel in the following conversation—

Well, Cooper, glad to see you again—you left us in a hurry.

"Yes," I replied, "It was an unpleasant affair."

Never mind, John went on to say, *you are a martyr, every good cause has its martyrs.*

Mr. Powell, who was present, then remarked that he was the proper person to be put in prison.

Then you are a martyr by proxy, was John's reply, who then went on to say, *You have come ˈto a queer place now.* Thinking he might mean the cellar we were in, to which we had come on account of its darkness, I said, "What place do you mean?" *Why, London,—you can do no good here now; you may as well try to resuscitate a corpse, go right away to some new place. It's too late for Russia now—Brussells is too near Paris—my advice is to go to Berlin; there you will create as great an excitement as when you first came here—lose no time, go at once.* Thanking John for his advice we bade him ' adieu.'

About this time a paragraph went the round of the papers to the effect that the Davenports had renounced their spiritual pretensions and now exhibited as conjurors, "professors of a peculiar species of legerdemain." This statement purported to be made on the authority of the "Scotsman," but that paper simply said that persons need have no scruples now about witnessing the exhibition as nothing was said about Spiritualism. A paragraph appearing of the same tenor in the "Athenæum," I wrote the following letter to that journal, which the Editor had the honour and fairness to insert.

The Davenport Brothers.—In justice to Mr. Howitt and his "fellow worshippers," allow me to say, in reference to the paragraph on the Davenport Brothers, which appeared in your journal of the 31st. of March, that there is no truth in the statement that they have avowed themselves to be conjurors. The Brothers and Mr. Fay, in the most full and explicit manner, deny that they have ever admitted themselves to be conjurors ; and they still affirm that the manifestations which take place in their presence are neither produced by themselves nor by confederates. Mr. Fay has already contradicted the statement which appeared to his prejudice a short time since in most of the newspapers ; but few of them however, had the sense of justice to give his letter publicity.

I am sorry to add that other journals did not act so honourably in the matter, refusing to admit an explanatory statement, even as an advertisement. Among these was the "Times;" this could hardly have been expected of that journal, since it once asked for Spiritualism, "a full, free and impartial inquiry ; an exposure of the sham if it be one ; and a recognition of the truth, if truth be in it." How true are its own words "How often must a great truth come forth to light, and be received and overborne, and lapse into obscurity before it achieves general acceptation !"

CHAPTER XIII

Dr. J. B. Ferguson.

In making a brief sketch of the career of the Davenports in Europe I must not lose sight of Dr. Ferguson who enacted an important part in the little drama that excited for the time the attention of the world, and to whose tact and good management its success was much indebted. It may be well therefore to state here a few particulars respecting him.

Dr. J. B. Ferguson was until recently the pastor of a large congregation in Nashville, Tennesse, of which the present President of the United States was a member. Here his ministry was so successful that a larger building became necessary to hold his increasing audiences, and accordingly a new and handsome church capable of accommodating 5000 persons was erected and placed at his disposal. In a work entitled " Supramundane Facts in the life of J. B. Ferguson," published in England during his residence here, it will be seen that for many years he has been acquainted with the facts of Spiritualism ; and he was not the man to preach doctrines he did not believe in, or to withhold truths he considered desirable to be known.

M

His nature was far too honorable, bold, and conscientious for this. Accordingly when his convictions became matured by a lengthened study and an extended experience, he did not hesitate to proclaim them; which, as might be expected, proved distasteful to the majority of his hearers. Dissatisfaction was expressed, an open rupture followed, and in the end the pastor resigned his position and voluntarily gave up his right to the church which had been built expressly for his use. His subsequent connection with the Davenports may be best stated in his own words.

"On the night of the 26th of April, 1864, in company with a friend, I attended the exhibition of the Brothers Davenport at the Cooper Institute, New York. On the night succeeding, in company with five of my friends from the Southern States. I attended another exhibition at the same place. I had been for years familiar with phenomena and experiences of a similar character to those represented as attending the Brothers; and from the knowledge of this fact, my Southern friends were anxious that I should accompany them.

"Of the Davenports themselves personally, or as representatives of the 'wonders' associated with their names. I knew nothing. Of course I had often seen their names in public prints, but my attention to what was said either in their favour or to their disparagement had never been sufficiently attracted to secure any conviction respecting them. Accordingly, on my way to their proposed entertainment, in reply to a question of my friends, I remember to have stated that, if the Davenports were not jugglers or deceivers, and were really instruments through which man's allied nature to the invisible or spiritual world was reflected, we should receive evidence such as no candid man could refuse to accept. I also expressed a hope that one of my friends, who was a sceptic in the saddest sense, would receive the tangible proof of what he had heard me assert and defend for fifteen years.

"When we came to the place of meeting—the large lecture-room of the Cooper Institute, the largest in New York city--we found some thousands assembled. The entertainment—for such it may properly be called —opened, and a committee was chosen to secure the young men in the cabinet and report to the audience what occurred. I need not describe the manifestations, or their effect on the audience, as the New York papers gave graphic reports at the time, and have indulged in tiresome repetitions since. It is enough to say that I was convinced that the Davenports were no jugglers, and that the displays of power through them admitted of no explanation according to any known estimate of natural laws. I called upon the Davenports in private, and attended their public entertainments for eleven days and nights. My sceptical friend after the closest scrutiny, admitted that there was no clandestine mechanism or arrangement of machinery, and no sleight-of-hand in what he had so doubtingly and thoroughly examined. He is a man of the first eminence at home and abroad in discovery, and in the application of discovery in the most intricate and difficult mechanics, and in mechanical skill has few equals.

"When the Davenports appeared at Brooklyn, near New York, it happened that their representative before the public was absent ; and they, through their friends, invited me to introduce them to the public of the city of Brooklyn. In that city, at the time, I was solicited to meet the representatives of a highly respectable religious society, with a view to becoming their pastor. I, however, consented to introduce the Davenports in "the City of Churches." I did this in a spirit of candid enquiry and experiment respecting a subject which I hoped might prove of interest. I did so knowing that, however desirable it might be that I should become the pastor of the church above-mentioned, my action in this matter would put an end to all hope of such pastoral charge being entrusted to me. I did so because I was fully convinced that the phenomena which occurred in the

presence of the Brothers was a part of the supra-mun-
dane evidence given to this age—evidence not to be
measured by the conventional restrictions of time and
men, however respectable the time or however religious the men.

"When I saw and knew, for myself and not by
another, that the evidences given through the Davenports were true, I accepted a proposition to accompany
them to England and Europe—if, after three or four
months' experience with them before the public, I
should find the work such as I could perform without
detriment to them or to myself. Accordingly, I spent
three months in the interior towns and cities of New
York State and New England, and a month in the
chief cities of Canada. During this time they were
brought before every class of the communities they
visited ; every conceivable form of fastening and other
methods of 'test' and trial were submitted to—such
as being held by the hands and feet while the manifestations of force were witnessed, the use of sealing-
wax, and many other devices--and always with
complete and undeniable success. Indeed, it were
impossible for me by any use of language too strongly
to state this fact.

"During this time I resided with them at the
same hotels, and we often occupied the same suite of
apartments. I travelled with them, in the unavoidable
intimacy of travelling companionship, over thousands
of miles of the wide-spread territory referred to, and
consequently must have had every opportunity of
detecting fraud, if fraud there were to be detected.
But it becomes me to say that I never detected any,
nor the appearance of any. When they were, to all
appearance, sound asleep, some of the most marked
of the manifestations have occurred. In travelling by
rail, when entering a dark tunnel, I have, to a mental
wish, received them in tangible and unmistakeable
forms ; and this experience has been repeated in
England. For example, upon our arrival at Liverpool, when we had taken our seats for London,
immediately upon leaving the former city, amid

expressions indicative of the natural anxiety of young Americans in their first observations and experiences as strangers in a strange land, on entering the tunnel near Liverpool, one of our party, I think Mr. Fay, said, " I wonder if John came with us over the sea ?" The question was instantly answered thus :—I was grasped by a strong hand, and so was each one of the company. At the same time that I was thus grasped, my face and hands were gently felt by seemingly human hands. I confess the evidence was so palpable and satisfactory as to distinctness of touch, responding to my wishes, that I feared some one of our party was the operator. I pleasantly charged them with it, when each solemnly protested he was the recipient of similar evidences, and had not moved, nor even desired to do so. I then desired mentally that I should be met by an evidence of such a character that it would admit of neither doubt nor denial. As we entered another tunnel I changed my position in the railroad carriage, so that no one of my party could touch me without my knowledge. In response to a mental wish I was touched, my face manipulated, and my person distinctly handled, when I knew positively that no one visible was near me. Of the satisfaction given by such an evidence I need not speak : no words can do it justice. I state the fact, and leave it to the appreciation of all who have the desire for similar evidences. I could give many other instances of force guided by invisible intelligence. On extinguishing the light in my room, I have had my chair instantly lifted and placed upon my head, with the legs upward, and the cushion resting on the top of my head. A voice—not mine, not that of anyone present—has directed me to feel the position of those present. I did so, while the chair held itself, or was held, firmly where it was placed. In distinct vocal tones I was invited to be seated, the chair being at the same time taken from my head and placed properly, that I might comply with the invitation.

" I might record a volume of such and similar manifestations. But with respect to all these evi-

dences, expressions, or demonstrations from the invisible
world, I have one remark to make ; I wish it to sink
deep into the minds of my readers. These are not
given in response to mere curiosity, idle wish or selfish desire. They have come when and where they
were needed, and where there was a degree of good
faith in the individual to use the evidence for universal good. The rule with me is, that whenever and
wherever the mind is ready for an ascent in actual progress, evidences are given that transcend all our
existing standards ef truth and good.

" For six months I have travelled with the Davenports, and in various conditions, advantageous and
disadvantageous, I have witnessed the evidences of the
power that attends them. I have seen them subjected
to every form of scrutiny that scepticism could devise.
I have seen their professed friends, with anxiety,
caused by a bigoted and sensuous denial, return to the
Davenports with fresh doubts, to be met and reassured
by evidences that admitted of no denial. I can truthfully say that no time, place, or condition of the most
diverse and promiscuous audiences, or the most select
companies, has ever prevented the manifestations,
though they have been rendered less satisfactory in
various ways. The anxiety caused the Brothers by
aimless discussion, captious criticism, and obstinate
denial is a very unfavourable condition. I have seen
them associated with persons who only wished to make
gain of their gifts, and whose methods of presenting
them to the public were calculated only to produce
distrust, and to place the evidences of the power
attending them on a level with ordinary jugglery.
I have seen these persons confounded, most unexpectedly to themselves, by the evidences of truth, wisdom,
and power attending the manifestations. Through
the most painstaking ordeals, the severest scrutiny,
the most searching analysis these evidences have
passed. They have ever come forth more clear, more
satisfactory and convincing to all honest enquiry."

When the Davenports went to France Dr. Fer-

guson accompanied them, but finding he could
be but of little use to them in consequence of his
inability to speak the French language, he left
them and returned to London. During the short
time he remained in that city he interested himself to promote the cause that lay uppermost
at heart and to which he had devoted his life ; and
rendered it essential service in many ways. His
commanding oratory had a magical effect on those
who heard his eloquent expositions of Spiritualism
in public, and his logical and affable manner in
private won over many to his views. However
humble the individual who sought information and
advice at his hands he received the same attention
and was treated with as much courtesy as the
high-born, intellectual inquirer. Amid all the
abuse that was heaped upon him and the offen-
sive epithets that were applied to him, I never
heard a harsh word escape his lips ; his feeling
seemed to be only that of pity for his calumniators.
To sum up his character in a few words, he is a
giant in intellect, a child in simplicity and an angel
in goodness, and one of Nature's noblemen. I look
back with pleasure to the time I spent in his
society, indebted as I am, to him for the high and
ennobling views of the work, and its ultimate issues,
it has been my privilege to engage in. The following letter by Dr. Ferguson shews his too partial
appreciation of my humble services in the cause of
the truth we mutually recognised.

London,—28th March, 1865.

My Friend, my Brother,

Your kind letter and its timely suggestions
are before me. At present it is not practicable for me
to appoint a time to visit Brighton. My relationship
to the phenomena attending the Davenports does not
allow me to make any arrangement for other perhaps

equally important duties, and privileges the knowledge of these evidences mutually awakens in minds alive to the cause of truth or right. But rest assured, dear sir, that I heartily appreciate your desire and the noble generosity of your intention respecting expences. If able at any future time to designate a night for a lecture at Brighton I will readily do so ; but I think, in common justice, it ought to pay *all* expenses and not throw an additional burthen on one already devoting all to the good of humanity. Nor can I write this sentence without adding, that amid the many seeming embarrassments attending the advocacy of the great principle we mutually recognise ; the ignorance, prejudice, selfish distrust we are compelled to meet in the gross and materialistic tendencies of the age, my mind turns to you and your exalted virtues and faithful labour, with a confidence and hope no language can express. Let one man bear his unbought testimony to your spirit in the work upon which you have so unselfishly entered. Its reward is not yet, nor here. It is known and recognised above the besetting currents of human feelings and expressions. No man in this realm, that it has been my privilege to meet, is doing more, or as much as you for a good that no time can measure or destroy. I shall carry its memory with me wherever it may be my privilege to speak or act for our common humanity. Disappointment may come in many directions to which your hope is turned ; but your work will remain and its great and signal benefits return to your own soul in the garnering hive of more auspicious times. Humanity is one and nothing done for good is ever lost. Receive my soul's best blessing and my heartiest fellowship ; for this I have ever felt towards thee and thine. Remember me to every member of your household. The spirit of love breathes over each and all, and holds its vigil for their unfolding natures in a trust not lost in death nor wasted on the desert path which mortals are treading.

With every sentiment of respect, thine

J. B. FERGUSON.

The proposed lecture to Brighton did not take place. I was just making arrangements for the delivery of two lectures in that town and in others by Dr. Ferguson, when a message from the spirit-world despatched him summarily to America to intercede in behalf of Jefferson Davis.

As a specimen of Dr. Ferguson's oratory I give the extract from his last public address made on an occasion of a testimonial being presented to him :—

A few months since I found myself, by a series of unexpected events, in your midst. It was my first visit to the mother country, but it was not my good fortune to make many and cherished acquaintances until during the visit now about to terminate. My connection with the Brothers Davenport and Mr. Fay is known to all before me, and doubtless to most of those who shall read these my last words to the British public. During that association, and the duties and responsibilities it involved, my heart has at times been pained by the untoward misjudgment we were called to meet : but more frequently has it been comforted, since, in a somewhat eventful life, I have learned that no truth is ever recognised by large classes of men save as it is seen to pass successfully through the furnace of passional conflict. Thus the lower, ever in the assertion of its existence and power strives, though it strives in vain, to bear down the higher; while, in the end, truth must ascend above all irrational opposition and justice prevail. Therefore, I have no fears for truth—none ! Let that truth come from where or how it may,—whether from the earth on which we tread, the elements we breathe, or the heavens from which descend light and love. Spiritual evidences I know must yet take their place in all practical, and especially in all truthful and religious minds. Mediums of every grade will do their work, and gradually the new era comes, when the great thought that spirit pervades and must control all forms of matter and all events of human destiny, will be recognised and acknowleged. As, therefore, I take my leave of you, I desire to say that it is the living consciousness of this truth that enables me to see in every man I meet a brother, inheriting with me a common nature, however diversified in its unfolding, and destined to meet and share a common destiny. This is no more true of you, my honoured friends, than of the teeming millions that make up the pale of humanity at large. The scavenger in the streets, the minister in the pulpit, the lord on his manor, the queen on her throne, and the labourers in your vast mines and extensive factories—nay, the very prostitutes of the midnight hour, of whom man is ashamed beneath the mid-day glare—the criminals in your prisons or on your scaffolds, are all equally dear, as they go forward to make up that family whose Father is One, whose destiny is the same. In the sight of High Heaven, I have learned to call and feel no man common or unclean. The Gospel which I bring you is for all, and its banner is held up by angel-hands over the so-called doomed and damned, above the gates of death, and its inscription, in lettering that all shall read, is—HOPE TO ALL. Consequently, with the knowledge of this relation of man to man and man to God, I can no longer be a mere Nationalist or Sectist; I can be but a man, and do the work that Heaven has assigned me, in the short time that I may dwell among the conflicts of earthly diversity. And I hope I shall not be less active or intelligent in any other world that may open before me.

CHAPTER XIV.

The Davenports in Germany.

I have already alluded incidentally to some of the most prominent inventions and discoveries that have marked the last half century. A little reflection will serve to shew their importance as auxiliaries to the Davenport mission. From seven months' experience of the working of the exhibition I feel confident in asserting that it would have been impracticable to have given these spiritual evidences to the world with any degree of success, but for the developments of modern science—the steam engine, the newspaper press and gas. The facilities afforded by railways and steam-boats enable the Davenports to travel all lands—a matter of primary importance. Before coming to England they had travelled over the United States and Canada; and since their arrival in this country they have travelled several thousands of miles, carrying with them their mysterious cabinet an' their battered instruments, with which they create more sensation than the band of a Costa. Their arrival in a new country is made known by the press and the facts are disseminated far and wide by its instrumentality ; and on visiting the provinces they have only to issue a notice a day or two beforehand and an audience is sure to be awaiting them. For the cabinet *Séance,* which can be witnessed by large numbers, a nice adjustment of light is required, and gas is indispensable on account of the facility with which it can be regulated. Thus we have an illustration how one step in the way of progress paves the way for another, one interest subserving the other—all tending, like the different parts of a machine to produce, by their united action, some grand and specific result.

Acting on the advice of our faithful friend John, the Davenports Mr. Fay and myself set out for Berlin, and forty-eight hours voyaging on a stormy sea to Hamburg, and eight hours' rail from that city brought us to the capital of Prussia on the 28th. April, 1866. Not being acquainted with the German language we engaged a Mr. Wohlgemuth, a Frenchman by birth and an exhibition agent by profession, to act as our business manager and conductor of the *Séances,* but unfortunately his acquaintance with "Deutch" was so slight as to render it necessary to read what he had to say. This, was of course a great disadvantage, and we were therefore obliged to let the facts speak for themselves.

On our arrival at Berlin, we took up our quarters at an hotel near the Railway station, until arrangements were made respecting the *Séances.* A difficulty soon presented itself which was altogether unforseen and unexpected. On enquiring for a public hall we found there was nothing of the kind in the town; all the large rooms being in connection with Hotels, and these could only be had at intervals. After spending about a week in futile attempts to overcome the difficulty, and at times almost despairing of doing so, we at length obtained permission from the king for the use of the private concert hall in conection with the royal Schauspielhausses, the Drury Lane of Berlin. This building is a large and imposing structure, situated in a fine open space between two churches, and is under the immediate control of royalty.

The night of our arrival in Berlin, William Davenport occupied a bed in the same room as myself. Soon after we were in bed, raps were heard on the floor, by means of which, it was signalled that the spirits wished to speak with us the following night. We accordingly assembled in the passage adjoining our bed-room as being the darkest place we could find; and soon had the satisfaction of hearing John's voice congratulating us on our safe arrival in Berlin. I jocularly remarked to John that he had an advantage over us – that he had no railway fare to pay. His rejoinder was *Yes, I've got no carcass to carry about— I get on better without it. My old bones are lying in the grave and so will yours be some day.* He then proceeded to give the Davenports some advice. *Brush your hair, curl your moustaches, black your boots and you will do well here if the war does not interfere. Don't go into the low restaurants.*

This last remark was in reference to the Davenports having gone, on their arrival, into one of the underground bars that abound in Berlin, for some refreshments. We spoke with him again a few days after and he expressed himself

pleased at our success in getting the use of the
king's private concert hall.

The first *Séance* took place before a company of
about sixty, assembled by invitation, composed of
members of the press, and other influential gentlemen.   Having been assured that English was
well understood in Berlin by the educated classes,
I prepared a speech for the opening night, but on
being told that not one in a dozen would understand a word of it, it became a debateable point
whether I should deliver it or not.   Ultimately,
acting on my own judgment, I decided on doing
so.   With the courtesy characteristic of the German people I was listened to very patiently
throughout, and although I was not understood
at the time by the majority of my hearers, there
was a great desire to know what I had said from
the few who did understand me.   It operated,
therefore, in the way I anticipated, and my object
was gained.   My address was to the following
effect :—

I commenced by assuring them that the manifestations, depended in no degree, on trick sleight-
of-hand, machinery or confederacy, the truth of
which had been proved by the most persevering
enquiries and examinations of the most able men
through the course of many years   I told them
how, that the ruder portion of the population of
both France and England, excited by their inability to detect the means by which the phenomena are produced, had occasionally lost patience,
and in England had more than once resorted to
violent measures.   Twice they had rushed forward, and destroyed the cabinet, actually tearing
it to pieces to discover secret springs, but they
had discovered nothing, for the best of all possible

reasons—there was nothing to discover. I said I felt quite sure that a people like the Germans, who possess the highest reputation for the depth and accuracy of their scientific enquiries, would give to these phenomena that calm and philosophic attention which they deserved; and whilst entertaining our own private views of the origin of these phenomena we desired to put forward no theory but permitted the spectators of them to draw their own conclusions; that they were *bona fide* facts was all we cared to establish.

In conclusion I alluded to the coat experiment, which demonstrated the wonderful fact, that under the agency productive of these manifestations, matter does and can pass through matter without leaving a trace of its passage, and commended its consideration to the attention of scientific men as one of great interest and importance.

The room in which the exhibition took place was fitted with a stage like a theatre and the first manifestation that took place was the horn being thrown into the orchestra; this was followed by one of the bells being propelled with such force as to go among the audience without any regard for their heads. Upon this, several gentlemen mounted the stage and examined the fastenings, which they reported to be secure. Surprise and bewilderment were expressed on the faces of all present. A well known gentleman (the proprietor of Kroll's gardens) entered the cabinet, and, on coming out, asserted that the Brothers had not moved in the slightest degree, which increased the mystery; and when a long naked female arm appeared at the cabinet window, causing a sudden exclamation from a lady, a look of terror seemed for the moment to pervade the countenances of the spectators. It was amusing to see the numbers, not only on the first night but on the succeeding nights, who examined minutely the machinery at the wing for working the gas lights supposing it it to be the mechanism by which the wonders of the cabinet were produced.

The Dark *Séance* followed, which strengthened the impression produced by the cabinet *Seance*, and a good deal of speculation was the result; but although there was an indisposition to admit a supernatural agency, every one evidently felt that he had seen something that could not be accounted for on any known principle of natural law —something more than was dreamed of in his philsophy. Herr Ganz, Chapel master to the King, gave it as his opinion that the Davenports could not have played all the instruments even if they had been untied. A favourable impression had obviously been made, and in due time long and excellent notices of the *Séances* appeared in the various Journals (seventeen in number) and this too, at a time when they were filled with news relating to the approaching war, almost to the exclusion of every other subject. This was considered a great point, for what the Berlin critics endorse passes current throughout Germany. A prosperous career therefore seemed before the Davenports, and they look forward not only to re-establish their *prestige*, but to recover the losses they had sustained in England and France, for contrary to general belief they had not been successful in a pecuniary point of view since they left America. On their first arrival in England, it is true, a considerable sum was realised by the exhibition, but the Davenports did not get the benefit of it. In Ireland,

owing to the poverty of the country, they barely
paid their expences ; in Edinburgh only, was there
an exception to the general unremunerative character of the *Séances* since the ruptures at Liverpool
and Huddersfield. But the expectations raised by
the preliminary success at Berlin were doomed to
remain unrealised. On the first night of opening
to the public there was but a small audience,
and on the succeeding nights still less, and so on.
This was attributed at first to the prices, which,
though less than half that had been charged in
London and Paris were said to be higher than
the Berliners were accustomed to, and they were
accordingly lowered to the Berlin standard but even
then the public did not attend in force, and we at
length discovered that the war was the all-absorb-
ing subject that engrossed the attention of the people. A consultation with the spirits therefore
took place, when I said. " Well John, we are
not getting on much." *No*, he replied, *it is the
war that keeps the people from coming—they can
think of nothing else ; besides it has driven all the
best people away from the town. You do not understand the language of the country and therefore are
not able to judge to what an extent the excitement prevails. You fixed the prices too high at first when the
interest was at its height. But you have done right
in lowering them—they are not used to such high
prices here.*

I then said with reference to the war "Do you
think it will come to fighting ?"

*Yes, there is no doubt of it, but it won't last long :
things are in such a complicated state in this country,
that each party is almost afraid to move, but it will
come to war nevertheless, it's gone too far to be prevented.*

It did not require a knowledge of German or a

N

ghost to come from the grave to tell us that the expected war was the great business of the day—the
one theme that predominated over every other;
this was visible in the military aspect of the town
and was seen written in the countenance of its inhabitants ; still we could not have supposed it
would have operated so detrimenaly to our interests
as was the case. It was some satisfaction however,
to find that we were not alone in this respect ;
every place of public amusement was deserted .
Indeed, a feeling of jealousy existed among the
various *entreprenneurs*, that we were patronised to
the extent we were.

During my stay in Berlin I looked into the
theatres occasionally, and it was no uncommon
thing to see more people on the stage than in the
house.   But although we were better patronised
than our neighbours, the *Séances* could only be
carried on at a loss, and we frequently resorted to
the spirits for advice under the circumstances ; and
they too, sometimes manifested their desire to communicate with us, and on one occasion said we did
not consult them often enough.   I have frequently
noticed that the Davenports acted as though they
were conferring a favour on the spirits by listening to what they had to say ; at any rate they never
seemed inclined to put themselves to any incon-
venience for the purpose.   One night we had just
returned from the Schauspielhaus when I noticed
that the table tilted : this I took to be an intimation that the spirits wanted to communicate.   I
proceeded at once to the adjoining room, and, finding it to be tolerably dark, returned and requested
Fay to accompany me.   On our going into the
room again, Fay proceeded to get a chair for
himself, and, while he was doing so, one was

brought for me by the spirit. Being seated, a voice commenced talking, urging me not to discontinue the *Séances*. It continued speaking with us for at least ten minutes, and telling us not to be discouraged, bade us 'good night,' adding *God bless you*. During the entire conversation every word was clearly articulated. The voice was that of a female, entirely unknown to me, and even the accent was unfamiliar to me : and were I not assured to the contrary, I might have supposed a woman had been standing by my side talking to me, so natural and real were the whole circumstances.

A few days after an incident occurred of an amusing character. One morning happening to be at the Schauspielhaus with Fay, I proposed that we should get into the cabinet and have a "talk with John." (this is the usual phrase of the Davenports.) Fay assented and entered the cabinet, taking his seat on one side; I followed and sat opposite him, at the same time pulling the centre door to. I then reached my hand to the bolt to fasten the door, and to my surprise felt a hand anticipating me in the act. The horn was immediately in motion and Kate's well known voice was heard speaking through it. She had not said half-a-dozen sentences when voices and footsteps were heard at the other end of the hall, and we soon found them making for the stage. The curtains of the room were all drawn and the place was in a state of semi-darkness. We soon discovered the party to consist of the man in charge of the theatre and two gentlemen, whose object was to make a private examination of the cabinet. As they were coming on the stage Kate said *Sit still, they won't be long.* The next minute they were banging the cabinet all round with their fists, and they then attempted to get it open; failing in this, there was an increase in the jabbering. In the midst of this Kate tapped me on the knee and said in a whisper *Sit quiet*. Finding they could not get the doors open, one of them put his arm in the window and tried to reach the bolt, but in this he did not succeed. A great talking continued and renewed efforts were made to get the cabinet open, and, as force seemed likely to be resorted to, Fay, acting impulsively, drew the bolt and the door flew open. Our besiegers drew back, startled and overcome with surprise, for they had not the least idea of anyone being in the cabinet. No explanation being given they doubtless considered that we were concealed in the cabinet for private practice. I afterwards asked Fay whether he bolted the door when we got into the cabinet. "No" he said, "I left that for you to do."

In Berlin, as in other places, the conjurors were on the *qui vive*, and sought to profit by the reputation of the Davenports. There was one at the Rappo Theatre who proposed as usual to do more than they did. He attracted the public by means of sensational posters representing a cabinet surrounded by sprites and demons. These we were informed were imported from Paris and were the same as used by Robin in that city. I did not attend the performance at the Rappo Theatre but was told that it was even a more absurd affair than Anderson's or Tolmacue's. I once witnessed this last gentleman's performance and was surprised to think that any person with a spark of judgment could for a moment place his performance in competition with the Davenport exhibition. I will briefly describe what I witnessed.

The performer was first tied with a rope considerably larger and stiffer than those used by the Davenports and in an entirely different manner to that in which they are generally tied, the wrists being perfectly free. He was then placed, seated on a chair, behind a screen with some instruments at his feet which he at once began to kick about. In about five minutes. having managed to extricate one arm, he put his hand through a slit in the screen : after another interval he was enabled to expose his other hand. He then attempted to throw a tambourine over the screen, but instead of doing so threw it against a chandelier which hung over head, causing a shower of broken glass—a manifestation not in the Davenport programme. Being now free from his rope, he made a great noise behind the screen and then coolly walked forth claiming to have done all the Davenports did. Such is the exhibition I witnessed ; and this trumpery affair was put forth as an explanation of the Davenport mysteries, and then used as a pretext by the *Morning Star* for refusing to do justice to the Davenports. " We will admit nothing " said the editor " in favour of Spiritualism, for Tolmaque does all the Davenports do." Those who take up this position must be either devoid of judgment or allow their prejudices to blind their judgment to such an extent as to render them incapable of perceiving facts. They observe through a perverted medium, the wish is the father of the thought, and they become the most unreasonable of reasoners and credulous among the incredulous! In the case of Robin, at Paris, the musical instruments were played by assistants in the wings, and the whole affair was a transparent absurdity—a mere burlesque to excite laughter.

We had pressing invitations from two or three

theatrical managers to give the exhibition at their
theatres. These gentlemen only looked at the
matter with managerial eyes, thinking it might be
the means of drawing the public to their deserted
houses. They offered very fair and liberal terms,
but ' John ' did not advise our going to the theatre,
saying it was desirable to avoid such places if
possible—that, being a supernatural exhibition,
it should be kept above the level of ordinary exhibitions. Concurring with his views we did not
entertain the proposals that were made. In
this we were blamed by our business agent who,
being in the profession himself, looked at the matter only in a business light. It seemed strange
to me, past comprehension, that this man although
he nightly witnessed this exhibition and even conducted it, could not realize the real nature of it ;
all he would admit was, that it was "something
he could not account for." I concluded therefore
that his head was not of the right shape to comprehend the subject. A little unpleasantness arose
with him once, when, to annoy me, he told a
gentleman, who was much interested in the matter,
that it was not spiritual, for he had been connected with some young men in Paris who could do
the same things. This report came to my ears and
in a very unpleasant manner. In the course of
conversation I was advocating the truth of spiritual facts, when I was met with the remark " Why
even your own manager says it is nothing but conjuring &c." I was of course annoyed, and took
an early opportunity to remonstrate with him,
pointing out that what he said, from his connection
with us, carried great weight. The spirits also
took up the subject, saying that although they
did not wish it to be put forward as " spiritual "

they objected to its being represented as anything else, and made this singular remark *If it is persisted in we will not give the manifestations, we can employ our time better.* Thus the matter ended, but although he remained with us for three months after this, he would never acquiesce in the spiritual theory. I remarked to John once, "I suppose Wohlgemuth can only see his salary in this concern. *You are mistaken*, he replied, *he thinks about it a good deal, he does not know · what to make of it*;" and on one occasion when we suspected he was not quite right in his accounts I said to John " What is your opinon of Wohlgemuth "? His answer was "*I think better of his hnoesty than his judgment*," and John was right as the sequel proved.

During our stay in Berlin which lasted about a month we received kind and courteous treat ment on all hands. There was of course the usual average of gentlemen more knowing than their neighbours, who adopted various cunning devices to "find out the trick," but in no place that I visited were we so free from annoyances, such as striking lights, as at Berlin. Members of the Royal Family occasionally witnessed the exhibition from the private box and on one occasion the King was present for a short time. There was some talk of a *Séance* at the Palace, but the war was just on the point of being actualised, and in consequence the *Séance* did not take place. We paid a visit to Potsdam when the use of the theatre was granted us by the King, and returning to Berlin to give a Farewell *Séance*, we bade adieu to the city with its Unter den Linden, its group of palaces, its stuccoed houses and its open-sewered streets.

CHAPTER XV.

The Davenports in Hamburg.

We next visited Hamburg. In this city resides
Baron Holmfeld, a friend to our cause, who does
not shrink from openly avowing his belief in
Spiritualism and the Davenports, and has stood
up for them through evil and good report.   This
gentleman had witnessed their exhibition in
London and had written long accounts respecting
it in the Hamburg papers which created quite a
sensation at the time ; we therefore considered
that the way had been paved for a great success in
this large, important and wealthy city.   Previous
to leaving Berlin we communicated with the
Baron informing him of our intended visit to
Hamburg, and requested him to have preliminary
notices inserted in the papers.   This he did, and
not having had our experience, announced the
exhibition as one of a spiritual character, at least,
he implied as much by the use of the term " unknown forces."   The effect of this was soon
apparent.   People came prejudiced against the
subject, and the press, to pander to the popular
feeling, spoke disparagingly of the *Séances*, and

advised the public not to countenance the spiritual humbug.   Another circumstance operated
against us.   The Baron undertook to deliver an
address at the *Séances,* and in so doing, put the
exhibition entirely on a spiritual footing.   This,
coupled with the fact that he was a great political
partizan and moreover not very popular, tended
materially to damage our cause, and the result
was that our *Séances* were even worse attended
than at Berlin.   Hamburg from its propinquity
to Schelswig naturally partook of the war excitement that prevailed throughout Germany ; this,
and the habits and character of the people, with
the causes already suggested, fully account for
our want of success.   Perhaps it would be difficult to find a town on the continent more involved in sensuality and worldliness, more intent on
physical gratification, more wholly opposed to
anything of a spiritual nature,   and yet
standing in greater need of these evidences than
Hamburg ; it is not the whole but the sick that
require the physician.   In reply to my enquiry,
" What was the prevailing religion there?" the
Baron's answer was " Mammon!"   Here a sight
presents itself that is a disgrace to civilization and
a blot on humanity.   Whole streets are devoted
to the " social evil," where its victims sit at the
windows throughout the day, showily dressed,
like goods for sale.

Our want of success induced us to seek frequent
counsel of the spirits.   John's discernment did
not fail to perceive the causes that were opera-
ting against us, and these afforded him a theme
for conversation. *You have not managed things
well here; you can do nothing if you have the press
against you; as for the people, they are three hun-*

dred years behind. *If you were to provide a barrel
of beer and some Polony sausages they'd come fast
enough, but they can't appreciate anything of this
kind.* Kate then began talking, passing remarks
upon the Hamburg people that were by no means
complimentary. She suddenly said *I must go,
here comes a nasty fellow, strike a light,* and,
whilst doing so, a pillow from the bed at
the opposite side of the room was thrown amongst
us.

We remained in Hamburg nearly three weeks
and having engaged the large Convent Hall continued our *Séances* during the greater portion of
that time although they were attended with considerable loss. Our term for the hall having
expired, the Baron kindly endeavoured to get a
reduction made in the rent; in this he ultimately
succeeded but not without considerable trouble.
This matter concluded, I proposed that the Baron
should have some conversation with the spirits as
he had never heard them speak, except on one
occasion at a dark *Séance,* when John said *How do
you do Baron.* For this purpose, as it was a bright
sunny day, I had the cabinet covered to exclude
the light; this done, Fay and the Baron entered
the cabinet while I remained outside. In less
than a minute, I heard John's gruff voice addressing the Baron in the following words, *Well,
Baron, I am glad to find you take an interest in this
matter.* The Baron replied that he was pleased
to have the opportunity of being of service in so
important a cause. John then alluded to the
business in which we had been engaged—the
settlement of the hall, saying *You had tough work
with the Dutchman.* After a few more observations he said it was not dark enough for him to

talk any more, but if we would have the room
properly darkened he would come and talk to us
at night. He then bade us "good morning."
During this time, he occasionally spoke to me as
I stood outside the cabinet.

In accordance with the suggestion of John to
darken a room at night, we went to the Baron's
residence. The Baron and I having hung a cloth
at the window to exclude the light from the street,
intimated to the mediums that we were ready,
upon which they came into the room, but almost
before either of them had entered it, the horn,
which was lying on the table, was thrown
in the air and fell on the floor. We then took
our seats and Kate immediately began talking in
a jocular strain; among the things she said to the
Baron was *The older the buck the harder the horn*,
implying, as we took it, that though he was
getting into years he possessed good stamina.

The following is an account of the *Séance* as
given by the Baron :—

The want of interest and attention, as to the
manifestations, in this town may be worth observation and reflection, because it shows the low degree
of spiritual interest in Germany throughout, and how
little expectation may be fostered as to the actual
and speedy development of Spiritualism in the great
fatherland of scepticism. Nevertheless, during this
depressed state of spiritual action in Hamburg,
manifestations occurred worth the liveliest attention
and consideration. Both the spirits, which take the
most active part in the manifestations, the male
spirit, Henry Morgan, and the female spirit, Kate,
represented as being his wife, entered into repeated
and regular conversations not only in the cabinet or
in the *Séance*, but in a darkened room at my house.
After a short meeting in the cabinet, the spirit
addressed as John King, told me himself, that in the

evening he would give more ample communications, providing the room was made darker than the cabinet then was (early in the afternoon), and when we met in a properly darkened room I immediately felt the trumpet floating in the air and heard the voice addressing me with great distinctness and force, and turning itself to other gentlemen when addressing them. When asking a question the answer was ready at hand, nearly before the last word *of the question had sounded, and Kate generally took up the topic, making her remarks often with fun and puns. I asked John King, how he could account for the indifference of the public in Hamburg. He answered, *the people here are two hundred years behind their time ; they are most material and don't pay attention to spiritual things. They won't hear about "geister,"* Kate adding the remark *they call it "spook."* We asked, "What is the aim of your manifestations ?" John King answered :

There is only one aim, one object in view, to convince men they have immortal souls. If they come here people are much the same as they were before, and you may fairly tell them, that as the tree is felled so it remains ; only there is progress. I am commissioned to do these things and there are those who direct me. Angels are seen, but far off, on high, and distinguished by a bright light.

Thus he entered into sundry spiritual matters, promiscuously interrupted by talkative Kate. When asked whether the ladies might be invited to converse with him, he had some objections on account of their talk. He admitted them, however, and began his communications by taking hold of a basket with shells, and expressing his satisfaction in finding and handling them. He threw them at the ladies and hit them with great exactness and continued the conversation for a quarter of an hour, responding to every question and interpellation, ending with a hearty 'good night' just as if he was exhausted or tired. But Kate did not come forward in this mixed company, and howsoever prone she before had been to speak and make jokes, she now had wrapped herself up in silence.

It may be well here to state that though *Henry Morgan* is the real name of the spirit, the Davenports generally call him *John King*, which was the name he first gave as symbolical of power. In the course of the *Séance* recorded by the Baron, in reply to a question of mine John said he was commissioned to do these things and that he got well paid for it, but I could not elicit in what way.

The time for leaving Hamburg having arrived our future course became the subject for consideration. The Davenports, and Mr. Fay in particular, were for going back at once to America, but, as it was necessary for them to visit London to arrange some business matters, I suggested to them to make a halt at Brussels and when there, judge whether it would be worth while to give a few *Séances*. This course was decided on, and we forthwith left Hamburg, shaking, like the apostles of old, the dust from our feet against that city.

CHAPTER XVI.

The Davenports in Belgium.

I now approach the most interesting and satisfactory part of my experience—interesting on account of the many remarkable and curious incidents connected with it, and satisfactory as being the turning point in the career of the Davenports.

In the facts I am about to record will be seen more clearly than in anything I have heretofore stated that this exhibition of spiritual power has been designed by the spirit-world for the accomplishment of great and important purposes, and that the Davenports are mere instruments through whom the spirits operate; as Mr Fay once remarked to me, "It is not our exhibition, but the spirits'." The more I think of it, the more I am impressed with the wisdom displayed in it. I will just mention one or two points that occur to me. Evidence of certain facts is to be given to the world; people are induced from motives of curiosity to witness them, and though manifestations of supernatural power are generally productive of fear yet, none—at least very seldom—is occasioned by witnessing this exhibition. Then again, its being put forward as an exhibition renders all parties independent; all desiring the evidence being able to obtain it at a trifling cost, while the livelihood it affords the Davenports is their inducement to go from country to country to exhibit. Those who think that these manifestations are unworthy of spiritual beings have only to be reminded of the fact that inasmuch as the spirit-world is peopled from this, it contains every variety and phase of human character. As Mr. Howitt has observed, "Are these who play tricks and fling about instruments spirits from heaven? Can God really send such? Yes, God sends them, to teach us this, if nothing more; that he has servants of all grades and tastes ready to do all kinds of work, and He has here sent what you call low and harlequin spirits to a low and very sensual age. Had he sent anything higher it would have gone right over the heads of their audiences. As it is, nine-tenths cannot take in what they see." Such work would certainly not be very congenial employment for the higher order of spiritual beings, but the character of the work agrees with the character of the spirits who are engaged upon it, who appear to be about such specimens of humanity as may be met with haphazard in our streets by the hundred. Taking into account all the circumstances attending the exhibition, especially bearing in mind that the manifestations can always be depended on taking place when there is occasion for them, I do not hesitate to pronounce it one of the most wonderful events in the world's history.

At Brussels we met with the same difficulty, as at Berlin, with regard to a suitable room for exhibiting in, most of the Halls belonging to the different societies that abound in the town, and are

for the most part only used for purposes connected
with the immediate objects of those societies.   The
result was that a week was lost in fruitless attempts
to obtain a place for exhibiting in, the only one
available being a large Auction Room which did
not appear the sort of place that the class, who
are the usual patrons of the Davenports, would
care to go to. It became therefore a matter of deliberation whether it would be worth while to give
any *Séances* in Brussels, and after looking at it from
all points of view it was resolved to quit at once and
go to London.   A time-table was referred to and
it was found we were about a quarter of an hour
too late for the steam-boat that day; we were
therefore neccessitated to remain till the next in
Brussels.   Soon after we had made our decision,
Ira Davenport said he did not like the idea of leaving the town without doing something " Well "
I said " we will hear what the spirits say about
it to-night."   Night came and we darkened a room,
whereupon Kate commenced in this strain.

*So you are going to leave this place without doing
anything ; you are a pretty set of fellows.*

John then spoke.

*Cooper, you must not leave here without doing
something ; it's a very important place ; it contains the
crystallized superstition of ages ; besides there is
great agitation going on in political matters—a contest has just taken place between the priest party   and
the liberals which has resulted in favour of the latter.*

" Well," I replied " You know our difficulty ."

Yes, said John, *I am perfectly aware of that but
if you do nothing else, give a Séance to the press and
let the facts go before the world in that way.   My advice is to take the room for three nights and give a*

*Séance to the press and two to the public and you
will then be able to judge whether it is worth while
to continue.*

" But " I said " if it's a failure, I shall be obliged
to send to England for money to get home with."

*Never mind, don't let a great cause like this be
sacrificed for the sake of a few pounds.*

He also instructed me to draw up a suitable address for the first *Séance* in which I was to explain
the Paris affair, as it had had, he said, great weight
with the Belgium people. Acting on this advice
we engaged the Salle L' Orient for three nights
and announced two *Séances* to the public. In the
mean time I prepared an address for the preliminary
invitation *Séance*, which I submitted to John for
his approval. He expressed himself satisfied with
it but suggested the alteration of the word " phenomena " *Say nothing about phenomena* he said,
*They are much more likely to believe it is Supernat-
ural if you say nothing about it.* I remarked " It is
like gilding the pill," *Yes,* said he, *and it oper-
ates before they are aware of it.*

In the address I remarked that " For several
years the Brothers had exhibited in America before
all classes of society but never till they came to
England were they subject to violent and outrage-
ous treatment on the part of the public or to systematic misrepresentations on the part of certain
portions of the press. Why such should be the
case it was difficult to understand. It was but
fair, however to state that the press in many instances had given true and faithful reports of the
facts without attempting to assign a cause for
them, which was all that we desired. In Ireland
and Berlin and indeed in some of the London
newspapers nothing could be fairer than the notices

o

that had appeared, and all we now asked was that a fair and candid statement should be published of what transpired. After explaining the nature of the alleged Paris exposure I observed that at Berlin where we had recently been, and where we received the fairest and most courteous treatment, it was generally admitted that no adequate solution of the matter had ever been afforded, and that I need scarcely observe that had any fraud been discovered the Davenports would not have been able to continue their exhibition in the very countries where these occurrences took place." In conclusion I said " I have only to remark that I wish it to be distinctly understood that the Davenports do not appear before the public, as has been stated, as propagators of creeds but simply as exhibitors of facts. These they present without offering any theory. They prefer to allow the enlightened spectators of them to draw their own conclusions, and leave the decision in the hands of the public, of whom they ask nothing but fair play' of which they heard so much in England but experienced so little."

The hall in which the exhibition took place had an open skylight running the whole length of the roof and, as it was the middle of summer, the room was quite light during the greater portion of the evening. To obtain therefore the necessary condition of darkness, a large piece of drapery was suspended, tent-fashion, over the cabinet, and measures were also adopted to render the cabinet more impervious to the light by sticking paper over its joints. This is the first time I ever witnessed the manifestations in what may be called day-light; the precautions we took had the desired effect and there was no diminution in the power of the spiritual forces.

About forty gentlemen, most of whom were connected with the press, attended the first *Séance.* My address was received favourably; and evidently produced an excellent impression, removing the prejudices of some and preparing the way for impartial and independent observation in most of those present. The speech was delivered in French, by our manager. We were fortunate in having two committee-men of the right sort, quick and intelligent and disposed to do justice, both to the public and to the Davenports. One of these was a gentleman connected with the press, named Berend. I may here observe that a great deal of the interest in the cabinet *Séance* depends upon the committee. If these are sharp, active and intelligent men and thoroughly sceptical (their scepticism is of no consequence if they are honest,) the *Séance* will always go off well and produce a good effect. The spirits evidently take note of the committee and sometimes talk about them. For instance, we once had a man who was very troublesome; he would not comply with the directions given, and thought by the exercise of a little cunning to find something out. He would pretend to shut the door, and then suddenly open it and look in; this was a favourite device of his. Well, after the *Séance* I remarked to Kate, that we had a curious committee man. *Yes,* she said, *but there was no malice in him.*

From "L'Etoile Belge" I take the following account of the first *Séance.* After giving a description of the cabinet and an account of the preliminary operations, it says, according to my translation :—

"The two brothers with white neck-ties and an evening dress sat facing one another against the cabinet and were firmly tied by the committee to the seat, both feet and hands. The doors were shut, the gas put down, and in a few seconds they were untied. The cabinet was shut, and in less time than it takes to relate it, they were shewn tied again more firmly than before, the cords interlaced five or six times round the legs, and passing through the holes in the seat tied their elbows and their necks, and also ingeniously tied their elbows and their necks to their hands behind their backs. The knots, artistically formed, would do credit to a weaver (tisserand.) To these cords the committee added others to render them still more secure. Each endeavoured to effect the gordian knot. Berend, who had taken off his gloves to pull the ropes tighter, and in doing so, hurt his hands, which were only accustomed to handle a pen and a cigarette. The doors were shut and immediately the violin, the guitar, tambourine and bells, which had been placed in the cabinet, began to sound, and banged about making a frightful disturbance. At the same time hands were constantly seen, agitated, at the window, and from which the horn at various times was thrown with considerable force. The noise ceased, and the doors were quickly opened, leaving the two brothers sitting in the same position and tied in the same way. It was declared they had not moved.

Berend, who had been standing near the cabinet was perfectly astonished; his physiognomy and his pantomimic gestures showed his astonishment and that he could not understand it at all. A voice from the audience asked him what he had seen. "Ah ! I have seen nothing more than you," replied he. "On shutting the door I apparently saw a detached hand."

"But whose hand—to which of the brothers did it belong ?"

"I know nothing about it ; I tried to catch it, but it was of no use ;"

Applause followed. The two brothers modestly inclined their Yankee heads; and these experiences were succeeded by others, stronger and stronger, absolutely *comme chez Nicolet.*

Berend himself was shut up in the cabinet with them. His face did not indicate terror, which showed he had no fear of being devoured. He sat against the back of the cabinet with his face towards the door; his right hand was tied to the shoulder of the Davenport on the left, and his left hand to the knee of the Davenport on his right. He had placed on his knees a violin, a guitar and the tambourine; the bells were placed on the carpet; the doors were shut, the gas lowered and...... All at once the violin was scraped, the guitar twanged, the tambourine jingled, the bell chimed beautifully. It was a veritable chatter. The doors flew open. The guitar and violin were on the ground, the tambourine crowned the head of Berend, who was still seated in the same place immovable and still tied to the two brothers. "What have you felt?" he was asked.

"I felt the violin and guitar moving about in the cabinet, and a hand moving over my face, which I assure you was not agreeable."

"How was that done?"

I know absolutely nothing of it; I have seen nothing there but *du feu*, or rather I have seen nothing at all."

But what good would it be to recount the other experiences, the experiment with the flour in the hands, or the *séance* given in the dark by Mr. Fay? The phosphorised guitars which fly about round the room and on the heads of the company; the coats taken off in a few seconds by a man who has his hands tied behind his back. It is necessary to see these things to form an idea of them, and especially to believe them."

The above may be taken as a fair specimen of the criticism of the Brussels press; every paper had a notice of much the same tenour as the one

I have translated, and although public attention was much engaged with the war in Germany, which had now passed from a state of *posse* to that of *esse*, great interest was excited by the accounts of the *Séances*, and formed the principal theme of conversation, and, after a few days, it was no uncommon thing to see little groups of persons in the streets discussing the matter, as their actions and a few stray words heard *en passant* indicated they were doing.

The public *Séances* were attended with success, and induced us to engage the hall for six nights longer, at the end of which time we were invited by the proprietor of the Theatre des Boulevards to give *Séances* at his place. His invitation was accepted, and adopting low prices and engaging a splendid band of music which played an hour in advance, great numbers availed themselves of the opportunity to witness the manifestations. We remained in this theatre for three weeks.

ῥ I must not omit to mention that while we were at the Salle l'Orient we were visited by Victor Hugo. Receiving an intimation of his coming, we reserved the place of honour for him—immediately in front of the cabinet. After witnessing both *Séances* he expressed himself perfectly satisfied with the genuineness of the manifestations and said they far exceeded his expectations—in fact he could not have supposed such things to be possible. I believe I am right in saying that Victor Hugo, was, at the time, a believer in spiritual phenomena.

During our stay in Brussels, I had more frequent conversation with the spirits than at any other period, for in consequence of their remark that we did not communicate with them often enough,

I endeavoured to induce the Davenports to listen more frequently to their counsels. Some of these conversations I will relate.

After our success in Brussels was assured, I asked John how he considered we were getting on, *You are making an indelible impression* " was the reply," *it will last after you have left the world.* I said it was a good thing we stayed—that we were very near upon leaving—our staying being at one time most uncertain. John concurring in my remarks proceeded to repeat some lines beginning with these words;

> " Great God on what a slender thread
>   Hang   everlasting things!"

I said " Why John where did you learn that, it sounds like one of Watts' hymns ? " He replied *I learnt that many years ago when I was a boy at school; my name is Henry Morgan—I am a Whelchman.* Our conversation was cut short by a flash of lightning followed by a loud peal of thunder. *I must go now* the spirit said. Does the lightning affect you ? I asked, *It does not affect me, but it affects my conditions.* Silence ensued and a light was struck. On another occasion, nobody but myself and Ira present, Kate said, *Johnny is gone to Austria; he takes great interest in the war.*

I asked, " does the spirit-world exert any influence on the war ? "

Undoubtedly, was the reply *The spirits are at the bottom of it.*

Ira then said " Do you mean to say that spirits instigate such dreadful things as wars ? "

Yes; it is the only way of arriving at certain results. A war is just as necessary at times, to clear the moral atmosphere as a thunder storm is to clear the air

In reference to the same subject I once asked, whether some great end was contemplated as the result of the war and the manifestations, and whether the ultimate result of both was identical; to which I received this reply. *Some great purpose is doubtless had in view, but what it is I hardly know myself, and I do not know that I should be justified in telling you even if I did.*

At Brussels William Davenport purchased a little Italian greyhound. One night Ira and I were alone with the dog in the room. The light was extinguished and immediately Kate's voice was heard asking.

What have you got here? " A little pup " Ira replied. A noise was then heard as of a hand patting the dog, and the animal whined. I remarked, " the dog doesn't seem to like you."

No, it can see me.

" Well " I said " I had the idea that animals are more sensitive to spirit-presence than human beings."

Yes that is the case; they can see us, and so would men if they lived more natural lives.

I, hereupon, observed that I could not think what William Davenport wanted with the dog. *Oh he wants something to love ; it's natural for everybody to have something to set their affections on. Ira has got his wife.*

" Well " I said " and what have I got "

You—, you have got your children. My spectacles were then taken from my face and hereupon I heard Ira exclaim, " Gently, you are running something in my eye." I said, " mind my spectacles, don't break them," *I won't hurt them,* the voice replied. A light was struck and my glasses were found on Ira Davenport's face.

In reference to the above I may remark, that at our *Séances* at home I frequently noticed that our cat always evinced considerable fear when the spirits were manifesting. It would shut its eyes and endeavour to escape from the room; whereas at other times it was one of the most quiet and staid of the feline tribe, and ever disposed to make itself as comfortable as possible.

On one occasion I obtained the following answers to my queries. The spirit said " *Insanity is not the result of possession as some suppose, but is owing to the brain being out of order. It is then like a man having to work with a defective machine. The spirit cannot act properly through a disorganised brain. On the spirit leaving the body it is no longer insane.*

"Do you remember the events of your earth-life?"

Yes, more vividly than when here because our faculties are quickened.

"Have you, as spirits possessing a spiritual body, ailments like ours?"

No, all our ailments are mental and all spirits are subject to them; all are affected by conditions as in the earth-life.

"Are you happy?"

Not always. I am sometimes happier than at others.

"Do you progress?"

Yes; we have our teachers. A child entering the spirit-world becomes an adult and is educated as in your world. It is best for a man to live out his time on earth, because it is natural.

The above interesting colloquy is recorded from notes made at the time and is the longest of the kind I ever had.

While at Brussels we gave a *Seance* at the house of the Princess————. There were only about a dozen persons present but the manifestations were very excellent. There was a finer display of arms than I ever before or since witnessed; they came out in rapid succession, two appearing at the same time, and were of a peculiar pink hue. I have occasionally seen veins on the arms. At this private *Séance*, on the cessation of the music the guitar was thrown into the room. I was at the time holding a lamp in front of the cabinet and distinctly observed a naked arm recede from the guitar, and once on the opening of the door I saw a hand leaving the bolt. This proves that everything that is done in the cabinet is done by hands formed for the purpose. During the dark *Séance* the manifestations were very powerful. The ladies at first thought it fine fun and giggled tremendously, but before it was over they were wonderfully subdued and left the room, and could not be prevailed upon to return.

A *Séance* was also given before the members of the principal Literary Society in their large room situated in La Grande Place. The room was crowded with the *elite* of the town and much astonishment was excited. One of the committee while playing tricks in trying to seize the bell, had his face cut open with it. At the end of the *Séance* we were surprised to find the instruments smeared with blue paint which had been put on by the committee unknown to us. We observed several gentlemen examining closely the hands of the Davenports but did not know for what purpose. They had not the fairness and the candour to state the result of the experiment they had made.

In Brussels I met an English gentleman and

in the course of conversation I asked him if he believed in spirits. He said he used not to believe in them but was disposed to do so now. I asked him what had changed his views; and he then proceeded to tell me that a few months before he was in Florence, and whilst lying in bed one morning he distinctly saw his sister, who spoke to him. He said he felt alarmed and came over in a profuse perspiration, and, on recovering, tried to persuade himself he had been dreaming; but this he could not do, as the appearance seemed perfectly real and he felt assured he was awake. He went on to say that ultimately he might have persuaded himself that it was only a vivid dream he had had but for the sequel. Three days after he received a letter from England stating that his sister died at the time he had seen and heard the apparition. I know other persons who have had similar experiences; and who indeed does not?

After exhibiting a month in Brussels we determined on visiting the principal towns of Belgium. The first we visited was Louvain. Here there is a college or university and our audience was principally composed of students, about seven hundred in number. We then went to Liege, Namur, Charleroi, Mons, Tournai, Ypres, Bruges, Gand, Ostend, St. Nicholas, Lokeren, Antwerp, and Tirlemont. We also visited Lille and Roubaix, two French towns lying in our route. In all these towns, although the cholera and hot weather prevailed, both unfavourable to public assemblages, the result was satisfactory both with regard to the attendance and the impression made. Frequently would the spirits remark after the *Séances*, "It was a highly appreciative audience; you are making an indelible impression."

It will serve no purpose to enter into the particulars attending this provincial tour; it will suffice to record a few of the more noteworthy incidents that occurred during this period.

At Charleroi William Davenport was taken ill with inflammation of the bowels. He was attended by the first physician of the town, but, as he was a sensible doctor and did not prescribe much medicine, the patient was dissatisfied with his treatment and wanted me to telegraph to London for a doctor in whom he had more confidence. I told him I thought it was unnecessary—that the proper thing, in my opinion, was being done for him; and on his still pressing me to telegraph to London, I suggested asking the advice of the spirits upon the matter. In this he concurred. Accordingly Ira and I retired to a dark chamber and were at once in communication with Kate. I began by saying "What do you think of William —is it necessary to send to London for a doctor?" *Certainly not ; he is going on all right, he will be well in a day or two. He ate too much melon yesterday ; you are neither of you* (meaning the Brothers) *sufficiently careful with regard to your diet ; you do a great many things that lower the vitality. If you were more careful we could do more through you than we do. Fay takes more care of himself and that is the reason we can do so much through him.* I here interposed and said "Don't you think they smoke too much ?" *Yes, certainly ; it is a very injurious practice, every cigar you smoke you drive a nail into your coffin.* Ira said " Well Kate I shall have a good many nails in my coffin then." I think this advice had the effect of diminishing the daily allowance of cigars. William Davenport was well enough to be removed the next day, so that my judgment of the Doctor's treatment proved correct. On settling with the gentleman we were all surprised at the smallness of his fee. He paid three visits, one of which was early in the morning, for which he charged six francs. In London the probable charge for like services would have been as many guineas. The general lowness of price that prevails in Belgium, especially in the provinces, is doubtless the reason why we cannot 'compete with the foreigner.'

At Tournai there is a very fine Cathedral. This I inspected one afternoon in company with Ira Davenport. The attendant took us into the vestry and showed us a variety of robes which had belonged to former dignitaries of the church and had been used on state occasions; some of these vestments were large, costly affairs containing a great quantity of gold. From the Cathedral we went to the Theatre where our exhibition was to be given. The building being tolerably dark I proposed to Ira to get into the cabinet to " talk with John." We were no sooner in the cabinet than we had evidence of spirit-presence, and John's voice proceeded to descant on our recent visit to the Cathedral. *I was with you in the Cathedral,* said he. *I saw you looking at those robes. They should all be melted up and the gold devoted to commerce. Religion does not want such trappings. Churches have had their day, but their game is nearly played out.* " Are you satisfied with the manner in which the exhibition is now put before the public ? " I asked. *Yes, but I had rather you did not come to theatres if you can get others places ; being a supernatural exhibition you ought to keep above the ordinary exhibitions, but the principal thing is to get the facts before the world. I told you the exhibition would pay if properly managed, for it is a wonderful exhibition. We do not come to make you money, but we wish you to live by it.* On my asking for some advice the spirit said. *It is for you to do the material part of the work.— for us to give the manifestations, nevertheless we are willing to advise you where we can, but in some respects our judgment is no better than yours.* On this occasion John was the only speaker : generally Kate is the first to speak and I have known her say more than once, "John would come and talk to you but it is not dark enough for him

While at Roubaix a curious circumstance occurred. We had all gone to the hall to give the exhibition except our manager. He followed soon after and informed us there was great consternation at the hotel, in consequence of all the bells in the house ringing, which they could not account for. I went at once to the hotel to see what was the matter; I found the bells had ceased but the surprise they had occasioned by no means abated. I asked if the bells had ever rung in that way before and they assured me they had not; 'they thought it must be the devil.' The bells I found to be arranged in a novel and peculiar manner, electricity being employed to act on them. I took an early opportunity, when conversing with the spirits, to ask if they knew anything of the mysterious bell-ringing, when Kate at once said *I and another spirit did it.*

"But how could you manage to do it when the Brothers were not present?"

There was sufficient influence left.

"How is it," I asked, "that spirits can do things when there is no medium present as in the case of haunted houses?"

They can act through the magnetism that is retained

in those places ; there is no telling what some spirits can do ; some spirits can do much more than others.

" Can you make yourself visible ?"

Yes, but I am not allowed.

" John showed himself to the Davenports once, did he not ?"

Yes.

I then asked whether spirits could convey messages between America and England so as to save the necessity of laying down cables. They said it could be done but that spirits would not do what men could do for themselves.

While waiting for the conveyance to take us from the hotel at Namur, Ira Davenport said to me, " Cooper, I had a dream about you last night, of so vivid a character that I continue to realize every particular. I dreamt you were up in a tree holding a large black serpent by the neck, the body of which was coiled about the trunk. It was making desperate efforts to get free, but you held it tight at arm's length in spite of its writhing, and called on me to come and help you. I said 'I cannot get at you to render you any assistance.' 'Throw at it' you replied. 'If I do, I may hit you.' 'Never mind,' you said, 'I may as well be killed by a stone as by a snake.' Upon this, I got some large stones, and proceeded to throw at the serpent. The first two took but little effect, but the third hit the serpent on the head, producing a noise like the splitting of a board, and the monster relaxed its hold, uncoiled, and fell dead."

At night, after the public *Séance*, we had some conversation with the spirits, and I asked them if they could tell us anything about Ira's dream. The reply was :—*It was not a dream—it was a vision and is significant.*

" Will you interpret it ?" I asked.

The snake is Old Theology, which you have got by the neck, and is squirming and struggling to get free ; but you hold on, our blows are telling and you will soon see it dead at your feet.

" What does the first stone mean ?'' I asked.

Our coming to England: the rest let the future reveal. You began at Brussels on the anniversary of Waterloo, and are now fighting a battle which will be attended with greater results than even that. Our mission is to uproot superstition from the earth. Superstition is the enemy of all progress. Destruction must precede reconstruction. We are now getting the lever under and shall give it a prise some day. Good night! we will see you again.

This was all spoken in a clear and well-articulated manner, and is almost word for word as uttered by the spirit.

At Ypres a gentleman who holds a high position in the town called on us after the *Séance.* I proposed to Ira to let him witness some manifestations in private. Accordingly we three adjourned to my bed-room. Ira took his seat at the end of a table, resting his hands on it, and at his request our visitor placed a hand on his shoulder and held his hand. I did the the same the other side. On the candle being blown out, the horn, which had been placed at the farther end of the table, was heard to move and was then felt gently tapping our heads. A voice was then heard speaking through it; the candle-stick was then thrown across the room. A light was then struck, and the things being readjusted the experiment was repeated. A more conclusive test than this it is not possible to give. Any person may readily satisfy himself of the truth of these manifestations by taking one of the Davenports into his own private room, locking the door, and holding the hands of the medium. It will be found that a musical instrument, a guitar for instance, will be played upon in the dark and carried about the room. This is a test the Davenports occasionally give.

The proceedings at Antwerp are the only ones now remaining to call for any notice. In this town the *Séances* were attended with great success. We had the use of the splendid hall belonging to the Philharmonic Society, which was nightly filled with the *élite* of the town. A very curious incident occurred here. When the cabinet *Séance* was finished a gentleman exhibited his hand covered with some black composition. He stated that he had caught hold of the hands that appeared at the window and fully expected to find the hands of the Davenports black, but to his surprise such was not the case. There was a private passage leading from the hall to the room in which the dark *Séance* took place. In passing through this passage, during the interval between the *Séances*, I used to turn the gas down and talk with the spirits. After the incident just alluded to, the spirit said, *That was a very good test, you must get it publshed.*

" In what paper ?" I asked

In the Banner of Light.

On one of these occasions I said, " You did not give us much of a tune to night."

No. The fiddle broke down ; you must get us another fiddle ; we can't play on that thing, was the rejoinder.

At Antwerp a *Séance* was given at a private house, about twenty persons being present. The manifestations were very excellent. Great quietness prevailed and the instruments could be heard and, by the light of the phosphorous, seen, floating about the room at a considerable elevation and for a long time together.

I was one day walking through the Picture Gallery of this town when I observed a gentleman copying a picture representing some angels at the tomb of Christ. I said jocularly to the artist, "Do you consider that angels have wings like birds?" He replied he "did not know." I said "Perhaps you don't believe in angels?"

"I believe in spirits if that is what you mean," said he.

He then proceeded to tell me his experience in these matters. He said he was induced a short time before to attend a *Séance* out of curiosity, in the course of which three letters were given as the name of the communicating spirit, but which were not recognized at the time. The spirit expressed himself unhappy and solicited his prayers. The letters indicated were the initials of his father's name. At a subsequent *Séance* the spirit made further disclosures, which were to the following effect as told to me:—

"My father died when I was a child, my mother having died a few months before; it was represented that my father had died from grief at her loss, but such was not the case. He told me he had committed suicide, and this was not his only trouble; he had fought a duel and killed his adversary. Inquiries were made and the revelations of the spirit proved to be true. I continued to pray for my father's spirit, and he expressed himself benefited by my prayers. Such was my introduction to Spiritualism."

I had now been with the Davenports a considerable time and my affairs seeming to require my attention I determined on returning to England.

Before leaving I spoke to the spirits on the

subject. I told them I was thinking of returning to my home and that they, I thought, would now be able to do without me. On former occasions when I had talked of leaving they had urged me not to "leave the ship" (this was a favourite expression) but in this instance it was "Well go to England and see about your business and if we think it desirable for you to return we will let you know." I left. The Davenports went to Holland and from there I received a message from the spirits requesting me to accompany the party to Russia; but I regret that circumstances prevented me doing so. The Davenports went there and I think I cannot do better than give their own account of their successful career in that country. From Russia they went to Poland and thence to Sweden. The following letter was written by Mr. Fay who has been represented as exposing the Brothers in America, but who has been with them ever since they left that country.

Petite Moski Maison Gambs,
No. 6, St. Petersburg,
Jan. 23, 1867.

Dear Banner—A brief sketch of the movements and doings of the Brothers Davenport during the past four months may not be uninteresting to many of your readers. After making a tour through Belgium, giving public and private seances in nearly every town of importance, with the *most triumphant* success, astonishing the masses, confounding the learned and scientific, who in many cases undertook to explain away the mystery, the Brothers made arrangements for a tour through Holland. On the 17th of Sept., their first seance was given to the members of the press and about fifty of the most prominent and influential gentlemen of Amsterdam, preparatory to their opening a regular series of public seances. The press, as usual, when not influenced by the popular tumult, or the pressure of a *mob*, made voluminous and interesting reports, describing minutely and truthfully all the different manifestations they had seen, and commenting with great severity upon the violent and unreasonable opposition which they encountered in many towns of England and France.

The result was, that two days after, when the Brothers gave their first seance, they were warmly received by a very large and respectable audience. During their stay of three weeks, they gave about twenty public and private seances in Amsterdam, granting investigators every opportunity in private to examine and test the reality of the phenomena, and in every instance giving complete satisfaction. During their tour through Holland, they visited nearly all the towns and cities of any note, giving, in *all*, ninety public and private seances, and were always received by large and respectable audiences, in many instances the largest theatres and halls being so crowded that many persons were unable to gain admittance.

After their return to Brussels, they gave several seances in the largest and most commodious hall in the city ; after which they started on their journey to St. Petersburg, stopping by request at several towns on the route, and giving public seances, to immense audiences, always being warmly applauded at the conclusion of the manifestations. After a long and tedious journey of ninety hours, they arrived in this city, on the 27th of December, and immediately commenced preparations for giving a series of seances, both public and private. The fame of the Brothers having preceded them, it required but a verbal announcement of their arrival to awaken an immense interest among all classes to witness the wonders that occur in their presence. Invitations were immediately issued to all the members of the press, and a seance given to them with the most satisfactory results. Every journal, without an exception, bore testimony in the most vigorous and emphatic language to the extraordinary character of the phenomena. The following day the Brothers received as many as fifty visitors of the nobility, all anxious to make engagements for public seances.

Their first public seance was given on the 7th of January, to one thousand of the nobility of St. Petersburg, and, in consequence of all the seats being engaged in advance during the day, the hall was crowded in every part long before eight o'clock, the hour of commencing. After a searching and careful examination of the cabinet, ropes and musical instruments, by the committee, (one of them a *Russian Admiral*), the Brothers appeared on the platform, and were received with great applause by the audience. For two hours the manifestations continued with great power, the committee resorting to every means which their ingenuity and that of the audience could suggest, *to fathom the mystery*, until they were perfectly satisfied, as they afterwards stated to the audience, "of the integrity of the entertainment and honesty of the Brothers."

The next seance was given at the residence of the French Ambassador to a party of his friends, numbering in all about fifty persons of the nobility, including many of the officers of the Imperial Court. General Cassius M. Clay, our American Ambassador, and the Count Scroffenhoff, brother-in-law to the Emperor, acted as the committee, and both after a careful investigation of two hours, during which time they received the most conclusive and satisfactory tests, expressed themselves perfectly satisfied as to the inexplicability of the manifestations.

On the evening of the 9th, they gave a seance in the Winter Palace to the Emperor and Imperial family, by especial request of his majesty. There were present about thirty persons, besides the Emperor, Empress, the Crown Prince, and the Princess Dagmar. The manifestations were very powerful, and gave the most complete satisfaction to all present. By request of his majesty, several persons were admitted into the cabinet with the Brothers, one of them being the Crown Prince ; by his request he was tied and untied while iu the cabiuet, in contact with the Brothers, also receiving many manifestatious which convinced him of the fact that there was some power independent of the Brothers. The manifestatious continued for two hours and a half, and at the conclusion, the Emperor and Empress expressed their satisfaction with the seance, thanking us very cordially and asking many questions.

In all probability we shall remain in Russia until April, and then return to Paris to attend the great Exhibition. The Brothers, as well as myself, are somewhat anxious to return to our native country, but we feel hardly justified in doing so at present, as there seems to be no end to the amount of work to be done by us in Europe.

Yours truly,   WM. M. FAY.

CHAPTER XVII.

Concluding Remarks

It must be obvious to every one that a close intimacy with the Davenports would enable an ob-
server of ordinary intelligence to detect their
modus operandi if anything of the character of legerdemain were practised by them. In concluding
my experience I can truly say, that during the
whole time I was with them, extending over a
period of seven months, I never saw aught to indicate that they were anything but passive instruments, the manifestations being produced by a
power outside themselves. Indeed, I feel quite
sure they could not accomplish these things by
natural means without being detected every week
of their lives ; and I give it as my deliberate conviction after all the opportunities I have had of
forming an opinion, that their manifestations are
a reality ; if they are not, then all creation is a
myth and our senses nothing worth.

I have witnessed the manifestations in public
and in private ; in the dark and in the light. I
have known at least three hundred different persons enter the cabinet, not one of whom has as-

serted that the Davenports moved in the slightest degree. I have seen a light struck several times while the instruments were being carried in the air, but no one was ever found out of his place. I have known, in addition to the marking of the position of the feet, other precautions taken to ensure their not moving from their seat. I have witnessed several conclusive tests, some of which I have alluded to, proving beyond all doubt that they do not participate by their active agency in the production of the phenomena. The coat of Mr. Fay has, scores of times, been taken from his back in my presence, and Mr. Fay at the time might be seen sitting like a statue with his hands securely tied behind him and the knots sealed. I have seen coats of various descriptions, from a large overcoat to a light paletot, put on in the place of his own in a moment of time, his hands remaining securely tied and the seal unbroken. I have known the coat that has been placed on Mr. Fay so small that it could only with difficulty be got off him. I have known a coat that was first placed on Mr. Fay transferred in a moment to the back of Ira Davenport, whose hands like Mr. Fay's were tied behind him, and the most curious part of the proceedings was, that it was put on inside out. I have also known the waistcoat of Ira Davenport taken from under his coat, all buttoned-up with his watch and guard just as he wore it. It will of course be urged that these things are physical impossibilities. Such they undoubtedly are; they nevertheless take place; how they are accomplished we cannot, with our present knowledge of the properties of matter, even begin to understand. They of course involve the passage of matter through matter and therefore seem to

favour a theory that has been recently put forth
that what we regard as matter is only force. This
fact I consider the greatest marvel this age of marvels has witnessed, and instead of being sneered at
and derided by scientific men should engage their
profoundest consideration. I may also mention
that on leaving a room in which I had been with
Ira Davenport for the purpose of talking with the
spirits a chair followed me into the passage, myself
being the last to leave; and on one occasion whilst
sitting cross-legged in the front row at the **Dark**
Séance, I was grasped round the leg above the
ancle and forcibly pulled on to the floor

I have now finished my narrative, which is, for
the most part, a simple and unpretending record of
facts of a very unusual, and, I may say, very
wonderful character, so much so that they will
doubtless be altogether discredited by the majority of my readers. They are nevertheless true in
every particular, and in no instance that I am
aware of, have I drawn on my imagination or
exaggerated in the slightest degree. I do not
put forth this little book, like one of Dicken's
Christmas ghost stories, which leaves the mind in
doubt whether it is meant for fact or fiction, but
as sober, solemn truth. Most of the conversations
recorded are taken from notes made at the time;
the general facts which form the subject of my
book have been witnessed and are accredited by
thousands. Did these facts rest on my experience
only, I might perhaps hesitate in giving them to
the world; but as they are now fast becoming
recognized by the intelligent part of the commu-
nity, I do not scruple to publish what so many
beside myself have perfect assurance of. I make
no attempt to theorise or to draw deductions from

these facts; or to reconcile the more obvious deductions with the prevailing theologic views with which they may be considered to conflict;— this I leave for others, more able than myself, to do. My own belief is, that these manifestations are the work of disembodied human intelligences, and that they are made for some great purpose; and though such work for spiritual beings, may not be in accordance with our preconceived notions of such beings, or the evidence afforded by the manifestations of such a description as their alleged purpose would seem to warrant, still it is questionable whether a more effectual and suitable method could be devised of combating the hard-headed materialism of the times and convincing men that there is something in the universe besides matter. A knock on the head with a guitar by unseen agency is, to some minds, a much more effective argument than the logic of a Locke, and it is not for us to call that "common and unclean" which has been the means of convincing thousands of the reality of a spiritual world and will ultimately shake the citadel of materialism to its foundations. This is not the first time that things foolish in the estimation of the wise have been used to confound their presumed wisdom, and it may be that these derided and despised phenomena will ultimately be the means, in the hands of Providence, of revolutionizing men's thoughts and feelings with regard to their cherished theologies and philosophies and of inaugurating an era of progress in the future of humanity, in which shall be realized correcter views of the duties pertaining to this life, and of the nature of that higher life to come.

The age for damning, dogmatising, creeds,
  Thanks to the power of truth, has passed away ;
For man hath nobler thoughts and higher needs
And more exalted purposes to day :
From the Soul's garden he tears up the weeds
Of idle disputation and display.
Not words intolerant, but the bright array
Of generous impulses and holy deeds
Are the bright evidence of saving faith,
The best obedience to his law who saith,—
" Seek for *the Truth* inquiringly— nor fear
The guidance which from truth's great source
  sublime
Leads wandering man thro' the rude tracks of
  time
To that Eternity, where all is clear,"
                          SIR JOHN BOWRING.

www.ingramcontent.com/pod-product-compliance
Lightning Source LLC
Chambersburg PA
CBHW030120030726
47498CB00007B/2480